The QUEEN OF DENVER

The Queen
OF DENVER

LOUISE SNEED HILL *and the Emergence of*
Modern High Society

SHELBY CARR

Foreword by Thomas J. "Dr. Colorado" Noel

THE
History
PRESS

Published by The History Press
Charleston, SC
www.historypress.com

First published 2020

Manufactured in the United States

ISBN 9781467146494

Library of Congress Control Number: 2020931996

It is my business to entertain, and that is a very serious business.
—*Louise Sneed Hill*

CONTENTS

FOREWORD

As the Colorado State historian, a professor of history and director of public history and preservation at the University of Colorado–Denver, I have been fortunate enough to work with Shelby Carr on her prize-winning research on a key but neglected woman in Colorado history—Louise Bethel Sneed Hill. It is a rare treat to have a graduate student display such passion and dedication to historical facts and present them with such creative flair. Shelby is a shining example of why, after forty-nine years of teaching, I suspect my students teach me more than I teach them.

I have had the pleasure of watching Shelby Carr mature into a successful performer and professional speaker, writer and historian over the last four years. As a dancer, she has toured the world, performing in seven different countries. She has also performed as an actress, portraying historical women for the Halloween Tombstone Tours we conduct for History Colorado.

Shelby has also shined as an intern at the History Colorado Center—formerly the State Historical Society—and in the governor's office, where she worked as speech writer for Governor John Hickenlooper. She also served as a paid staff member at the Byers-Evans House Museum.

Somehow, she has found the time to also be very active in the community's civic and philanthropic causes. Within the pages of this book, you will get a wonderful look at how Louise Hill transformed Denver society. Shelby puts to rest many of the myths that have surrounded her life, including her alleged rivalry with Margaret "Molly" Brown, the "unsinkable" heroine of the Titanic disaster. Shelby's fresh, lively perspective brings Hill back to life. She captures the daring story of a woman living in a patriarchal time, articulating the transformation of gender, culture, class and consumption during the Gilded Age. Women of the Gilded Age have often been misrepresented or disregarded, even though they held remarkable power and influence. Louise possessed a unique set of social skills, which culminated from her southern roots, northern ties and western experiences. She was able to utilize the social facets that were common in each region to create an entirely new path for the city of Denver. A liberated lady, Louise dared to participate in an open affair and introduce her peers to the flapper girl behavior of the 1920s. In the pages of this book, Shelby will introduce you to this fascinating and important changemaker in Colorado's and women's history.

Enjoy!

—Thomas J. "Dr. Colorado" Noel

ACKNOWLEDGEMENTS

This book would not have been possible without the incredible assistance of my graduate school advisors, Bill Wagner and Tom Noel. Their guidance and suggestions on research avenues were indispensable. To the Hill family descendants: thank you for sharing your knowledge of your family history with me and for allowing me to share my research with you all. Much of the information about Louise Hill's early life would not have made it into this book without the assistance of Granville County historian Mark Pace. I would like to extend a special thanks to the folks at Haddon, Morgan and Foreman—the law firm that currently owns the Crawford Hill Mansion—and, specifically, Renee McReynolds for aiding me in my research process by allowing me to go through the firm's archival file on Louise Hill and her home. Lastly, I would like to give a heartfelt thank-you to my wonderful parents for their support throughout this process.

INTRODUCTION

A woman of short stature, high heels and quick wit, Louise Sneed Hill ruled over Denver's high society for four decades with her Southern charm, societal tact and passion for success. To Hill, elite society was, in part, a game that could be lost and won, and she was determined to come out on top. Much like the ideal of the self-made man, which implied success in a professional capacity, shrewdness and wit in business and the acquisition of great wealth, Hill was a self-made woman in terms of elite societal achievement. She aided in ushering in a new era of culture in the United States. She was one of the earliest women to publicly bring about the transition from a Victorian culture to a more modern culture that embraced things like alcohol and leisure activities. Hill's personality was, in the words of *Denver Post* reporter Helen Eastom, the culmination of "the delicate grace and dignity of the South and the charming vigor and spontaneity of the West."[1] She combined her southern roots, which stemmed from a relaxed, Victorian culture of leisure, with the morals and puritanical work ethic that were common in the North and the vision of liberal individualism that the West provided to present a new vision of American gentility.

Hill was born in a compelling time, between the Victorian moralists of the preceding generation and the flappers of the next. While the modernization of society is typically attributed to movie stars, celebrities and jazz age contemporaries of the 1920s and the following decades, the members of Louise Hill's generation were actually the earliest catalysts for change. Born in the 1860s, Hill, who had aspirations of leading high society, had to find a delicate balance between reconciling with the older generation and bringing about new traditions to satisfy the more modern, vogue-inclined individuals of her own generation and the following generation, who entered the social scene during her reign. Oftentimes, it was this uncharted middle ground that made so many of her decisions appear paradoxical. While she felt that much of society was too stringent, she still hearkened toward maintaining control and policing society; she felt that the reins needed to be loosened but authored a book on social etiquette. She desired an essence of strictness with playful qualities; she introduced animal dances (such as the worm wiggle and turkey trot) and championed the enjoyment of alcohol and other frivolous activities, like roller-skating, to the privileged class. Throughout her tenure as the doyenne of Denver's upper crust, Hill walked a fine line between the old and the new at a time when American society was unsure of its social direction as it entered the first decades of the twentieth century.

In Hill's time, high society was a "queer game."[2] Those outside of Hill's inner circle were warned by the press: if an individual was not prepared with the required skills to enter the arena of elite society, they were instructed to heed the warning and beware what they might encounter. Hill used her intelligence, ambition, passion and money to create a legitimate aristocratic-style high society in the city of Denver. She created the game and served as its master, arbiter and most-decorated player.

Hill's actions reflected America's shift toward modern society, as she fashioned herself into a self-made woman by consciously separating herself from her husband publicly and creating her own individual identity. Mr. Hill did not always attend society events with her, nor was he noted as hosting many of the events at their mansion. Much like the reality television stars of today and the early players and actors of the movie industry who helped publicly display society's change, Hill used the press. She gave interviews and party invitations to newspaper reporters in order to pull back the veil on high society. She wanted her audience to know how hard she worked in her role as a society leader while making it look effortless. She believed it was her duty and responsibility to lead society, and she believed that the role of a society leader was not only useful and important to the community but that it was one of the hardest kinds of work. She once stated that being a society leader was more difficult than being the general of an army, because "the society leader must manage women. And to fight her battles, she cannot use brute force. Tact is the only weapon she can use....She must always be alert and planning, for one wrong move may wipe her colors from the field."[3]

Hill believed high society required a particular set of skills (traits that she possessed) by which she could deem herself the ultimate leader. Based on the example of Mrs. Caroline Schermerhorn Astor of the "400" New York City Knickerbocker society, Hill armed herself with the tools necessary to achieve her goals. She was featured on the society pages of the local newspapers every day, emphasized drama in the upper class of society and even paid editors of local newspapers, like those at the *Denver Post*, to follow her wishes. Hill also used her words carefully to very publicly but politely set the boundaries of elite sociability.

Hill created a society group in Denver that was dubbed the "Sacred 36." The "little band" that "began with nine tables of bridge about whose edges gathered the ultra-ultras of the day's elite" comprised influential, wealthy Denverites, as described by the *Rocky Mountain News*'s society pages on April 22, 1934.[4] The Sacred 36, a reinvention and modernization of the "old guard" (a previously existing, informal class of the wealthy in Denver), was the first internationally recognized elite social scene in Denver and resulted in the acknowledgment of the city as a legitimate cultural and educational center to the larger world. The citizens of Colorado are still feeling the effects of Hill's work in Denver's social scene—how she aided in the elevation of the city to an international platform and made it a desirable destination for world figures and foreign dignitaries—as, today, the city continues to be well regarded for its abundance of cultural institutions. Louise Sneed Hill desired to become a dignified leader of Denver's elite, to elevate the city of Denver from a frontier entrepot to a refined and cosmopolitan city and to rejuvenate high society. These motivating factors led her to create the Sacred 36.

In a time when women were entering the public domain and culture was shifting to a modern society, Hill blazed the trail for so many who came after her. During the Gilded Age, the conventional role of bourgeois women needed to change due to the shift in industrial invention and the ensuing variations in females' roles and purposes within the private sphere. Hill was a pioneer in this social change and the alteration of purpose for women of her class. Her progressive thoughts and behaviors helped aid America's early transition from a Victorian culture that was driven by work ethic and in which women remained in the home and pleasures such as alcohol, games and sexual desires were censored to a contemporary culture in which women could establish their own identities, drink, dance, embrace their sexuality and enjoy leisure and fun without being deemed fallen women. She was a critical agent of change, and by studying her actions, behaviors and life, we can better understand the class formations, cultural consumption and gender during the Gilded Age. Louise Hill forever altered the path of the center of the final frontier and helped usher in the era of modern decadence, womanhood and leisure for leisure's sake in the United States.

Many historians have discussed the formation of high society in New York, and others have penned works concerning the modernization of Victorian society. Some have expressed how celebrities, gender roles and class identity during the latter part of the Gilded Age contributed to the overall shift of America into a more contemporary society, but very few have written about these subjects in conjunction or have attributed the modernization of society to America's first real celebrities, the wealthy individuals of the Gilded Age. Louise Hill has not received much attention from historians and has never been recognized as an early influencer of modern society.

Some historians, like Emily Katherine Bibby, have touched on the topics of class, gender identity and the roles of women in America's high society during the Gilded Age. In her thesis "Making the American Aristocracy: Women, Cultural Capital, and High Society in New York City, 1870–1900," Bibby suggested that the women of New York created and maintained their identity within the city's elite social circle by "possessing, displaying, and cultivating, from one generation to the next, cultural capital." She further explained her argument through a comparison of American society to English aristocracy. She claimed that, while English nobility gained status from who they were (their ancestry or lineage), American "aristocracy" gained power from what they did.[5] The exploration of the concept of cultural capital is important to my research, but more specifically, Bibby's discussions about the perpetuation of exclusivity are pertinent to my findings. I will not only expand on this topic but also offer a differing view due to the geographic variations of Colorado's and New York's societies.

Mary Rech Rockwell, in her article "Gender Transformations: The Gilded Age and the Roaring Twenties," discussed gender as a social construct. She wrote about the Gilded Age as a time when gender roles were changing and when women moved from the private sphere into the public sphere. She commented on how the women of the time challenged the old idea of their gender being "the weaker sex," a thought that had prevailed for centuries.[6] This point is particularly important when contemplating how women could assert their presence in and control over society. I intend to expand further on Rockwell's findings by asserting that these women were not only entering the public sphere but also taking control of their public images and influencing society into the modern era.

Historians have also discussed the transitional period between the Victorian and modern cultures and this period's chief influences. Historian Larry May, in his work *Screening Out the Past*, stated that movies and early players helped bring about the origins of mass culture in America and the "moral experimentation" of the twentieth century.[7] He also noted that historians have suggested that one of the most essential evolutions that occurred in the time after the American Revolution was the transition from a traditional to a contemporary culture.[8] May dates the early transition period from Victorianism to modern culture as 1912 to 1914. He attributed this successful transformation to actors, such as Mary Pickford and Douglas Fairbanks.[9] While there is no question that May's arguments have validity and that the movies and early actors aided in the completion of the transition to modern society, I would argue that there were other major influencers prior to his 1912 start date. Louise Hill and others from her generation were on the cusp of Victorian tradition and contemporary culture. Generally, we may not consider the elite to be critical agents in pushing the transition of American culture into its modern form. Overall, it is customary for us to look at later decades of movie stars, flappers and famous authors, like F. Scott Fitzgerald, as the real influencers. However, they would not have been able to accomplish what they did without Louise Hill and others of her generation, who had blazed the path for them decades earlier. Hill and others like her were, in fact, critical agents of change and fashioned themselves as America's first celebrities, a role that movie stars would fill for future generations.

There is also a lack of literature concerning the formation of high society and modern culture in Colorado. There is an abundance of information available that pertains to the formation of New York's high society, but there is not nearly as much research regarding the first elite social scene in Denver. The combination of the formation of Denver's social scene, its influences, changing gender roles and class identity in the West during the Gilded Age have scarcely been written about in conjunction with one another. With this book, I intend to shed light on not only the establishment of Denver's first elite social circle but also the woman who made it possible by influencing American culture to move into the contemporary era.

1

A SOUTHERN BELLE GOES WEST

Louise Bethel Sneed was born in 1862, into the southern aristocracy. There is some dispute over the exact date of her birth. While some sources cite that her birthday is in March, a diary of her aunt (Mary Jeffreys Bethel) states Louisa "Louise" Sneed (Louise's mother) died on July 11, 1862, "leaving an infant 11 days old."[10] An undated newspaper article—clipped and placed in a scrapbook that now resides within the larger Louise Hill Collection at History Colorado Center—entitled "Society Forecasts" claimed that Mrs. Crawford Hill was born on June 28 "in the sign of Cancer" and was "attributed with attaining remarkable prominence and power."[11] While there is no birth certificate for Louise Bethel Sneed, from the information provided, one can say with some certainty that she was born between June 28 and July 1, 1862.

Louise's parents, William Morgan Sneed (1819–91) and Louisa "Louise" Maria Bethel (1823–62), were lifetime residents of North Carolina. Louise's father's side of the family first appeared in North Carolina in 1761, when Louise's great-great-grandfather Samuel Sneed purchased a tract of land in what was then Granville County. Sometime between his arrival in the mid-eighteenth century and the turn of the nineteenth century, the Sneed family built a large plantation that was known locally as the Sneed Mansion, and the family members became prominent figures in the community.[12]

The plantation remained in possession of the Sneed family for generations. After many Sneeds chose to relocate to Tennessee, Kentucky and other neighboring states, the plantation in Granville County became the home of

Left: Louise Bethel Sneed, pictured here as a young woman, grew up privileged on her family's expansive property in Granville County, North Carolina. *Courtesy of History Colorado, accession #90.314.29.*

Below: Sneed's Mansion, pictured in 1955, is virtually unrecognizable today. Hidden by overgrowth and massive trees, the structure is currently buried deep in the woods. *Courtesy of the North Carolina Room, Granville County, North Carolina Library System.*

William Morgan Sneed and his family. According to the 1860 U.S. census, the Sneed property was worth about $12,920 (roughly $396,000 in today's currency), with William Morgan's personal estate totaling approximately $51,117 (approximately the equivalent of $1.6 million today). The Sneed Mansion was considered the "center of much gaiety, with parties, dances, horseracing, cock fighting, hunting, fishing, drinking, and gambling." According to local history, the reputation of the mansion was "far-flung," and when court adjourned in nearby Oxford, the common expression among the townspeople was that "court adjourned to Sneed Mansion House."[13] Williamsboro, the area in which the Sneeds resided in Granville County, was an important place in the state. It was an area that had a large tobacco industry, with plantations that grew the product and a factory that processed it. According to local historian Mark Pace, Williamsboro was even considered a potential capital city for the state. Williamsboro held an important place in the South, and as Pace noted, "there's a reason the Sneeds were there."[14]

William Morgan Sneed, like his patriarchal line before him, was a slaveholder. His father, Richard, owned twenty-five slaves when he was in charge of the plantation. When Richard Sneed decided to move to Kentucky around 1850, he sold a portion of his slaves to William. William married Louisa "Louise" Maria Bethel of Caswell County, North Carolina, on June 28, 1842, and they had six children together: William Morgan Sneed Jr. (around 1843–95), Richard G. Sneed (around 1845–around 1922), Mary "Mollie" Bethel Sneed (around 1849–1933), Lucy Henderson Sneed (around 1851–1907), Walter Alves Sneed (around 1853–?) and Louise Bethel Sneed, their youngest.[15]

Hill's young life appears to have been fraught with a bit of heartache. Her mother, Louisa "Louise," passed away in July 1862, when Louise was only an infant. In fact, her mother was buried on the same day that infant Louise was baptized. A newspaper article in the *Raleigh Register* on July 23, 1862, stated:

> *Departed this life on the morning of the 11th Mrs. Louisa Sneed, wife of Maj. William M. Sneed of Granville County, N.C. and daughter of Gen. Bethel, of Caswell county, in the thirty-eighth year of her age. A devoted husband and six children, the youngest only eleven days old, have seldom had the misfortune to lament so sad a bereavement. Possessed rare personal attractions, genial in disposition, cheerful and happy, with unusual vivacity… highly educated and adorned with every Christian virtue, the subject of this brief announcement had endeared to her all who knew her.…Let all who*

Above: The headstone of Louise Sneed Hill's mother reads "Louise Bethel Sneed—our mother." It is unclear whether newspaper articles and church records of the time were incorrect in spelling her name as "Louisa." It is possible that her headstone is incorrectly inscribed or that she was just called Louisa by those who knew her. *Courtesy of Shelby Carr.*

Opposite: The image on the top shows how St. John's fell into disrepair in the early nineteenth century, but it was carefully restored to its original grandeur, as depicted in the image on the bottom. *Courtesy of the North Carolina Room, Granville County, North Carolina Library System.*

> *knew her imitate her Christian forbearance and fortitude, and secure by the favor of God like her a blissful immortality in the world to come. Her remains now lie interred in the Episcopal church yard in Williamsboro, there to await the morning of the general Resurrection* [sic].[16]

Pictured here, in 2019, St. John's Episcopal Church can be seen on the right, and the remains of the Sneed Mansion are located inside the mass of trees on the left side of the image. The Sneeds' burial area (which contains the headstones of W.M. Sneed; his first wife, Louisa "Louise"; and his second wife, Sarah "Sallie" Sneed) is located on the land, in between the two structures. *Courtesy of Shelby Carr.*

The St. John's Episcopal Church register for 1862 lists that infant "Lou Bethel" was baptized to parent "Wm Sneed" on July 12. The register also lists "Mrs. Louisa Sneed" as a burial for that day. Although the newspaper articles and the church register list Louise's mother with the name "Louisa," her headstone in the St. John's cemetery is inscribed with the name "Louise."

St. John's Church was the chosen house of worship for the Sneed family, and it was basically located in the side yard of the Sneed's property. The front door of the church is mere yards away from the Sneed Mansion property. The parish (also historically referred to as Nut Bush Church) was established in 1746, the initial structure was built in 1757 and the church was moved to its present location and building, about a half-mile from its original site, in 1772 or 1773. St. John's is the oldest frame church in the state of North Carolina, and it is also one of three remaining colonial church buildings.[17]

Though tragedy was present in her early life, Louise's family name provided her with a comfortable childhood, and she grew up as a southern belle in the grand home on her family's land.

GENEALOGY OF THE SNEED FAMILY

The Sneed family was prominent in the South, and they strengthened their power through marriages that connected them to some of the most influential individuals in the South during the eighteenth and nineteenth centuries. Samuel Sneed (1723–1806), the patriarch of the North Carolina Sneed family, was originally from Virginia. Born in 1723, Sneed first served in the American Revolution as a captain and was later promoted to major. He first appeared in Granville County in 1761, when his name was listed in a deed transaction. He remained in Granville and was listed on numerous tax and deed records throughout the remainder of the eighteenth century. Samuel married Jane Dudley, also of Virginia, and they had approximately nine children together. In his will, which was dated 1800 and probated in 1806, Samuel named the executors of his estate, including his son, Stephen Sneed (1756–1821).

Stephen also served in the Revolution supposedly under famed general Daniel Morgan.[18] From the time of the war until he passed away in 1821, Stephen Sneed served as the first clerk of the Court of Pleas and Quarter Sessions of Granville County. In 1779, he married Mary Williams (1761–1826) in Granville County. Stephen and Mary had approximately ten children together.[19]

Stephen and Mary's son, Dr. Richard R. Sneed (1790–1861), married Lucy Henderson (1798–1868), the daughter of Leonard Henderson (a former judge of the superior and supreme court), in 1814.[20] Leonard was the son of the famed Judge Richard Henderson, a colonial judge who was born in Virginia and who was owner of the Ashland Plantation (the oldest home in Vance County).[21] Richard Henderson was also the cousin of William Williams (the father of Mary Williams Sneed). William's brother, Judge John Williams, owned the Montpelier Plantation in Granville County, where he operated a law school for a short time and studied with his cousin Judge Henderson.[22] In 1774, Judge Henderson was interested in acquiring lands from the Cherokee tribe and consequently founded the Transylvania Company to accomplish this task—an entity that both of his cousins invested in. The Transylvania Company hired Daniel Boone to explore the area they hoped to purchase; the trail Boone blazed, the Wilderness Road, "became the main route to the new settlements."[23] The company took possession of the Native American lands in 1775 and founded what would become the state of Kentucky. Though the governors of North Carolina, Virginia and Tennessee declared that Henderson's purchase was illegal, they all subsequently granted the company about two hundred thousand acres in lieu of their agreement with the Cherokee. Henderson subsequently set up a land office to deed and sell the lands to settlers.[24]

Dr. Richard Sneed was a physician who was "respected by all and beloved by those with whom he was brought into professional contact."[25] He and his wife, Lucy, had ten children, and their eldest was son William Morgan Sneed, the father of Louise Sneed Hill. The future Mrs. Hill grew up privileged and well connected. She spent many summer seasons with distant relatives and close family friends Mrs. Varina Howell Davis (the second wife of the president of the Confederate States) and Mrs. Worthington Davis (the cousin of Jefferson Davis and the mother-in-law of Joseph Pulitzer, the creator of the Pulitzer Prize) at the St. Elmo in Green Cove Springs, Florida.[26]

In 1875, Miss Varina Anne "Winnie" Davis (her name was published incorrectly in local newspaper articles as "Minnie" Davis), the daughter of "Great Jeff" Davis, visited the Sneeds and stayed with them at their Granville County home. According to newspaper articles from September 1875, Winnie, "a fresh and handsome young lassie," was "on a visit to the family of Major Sneed" and had traveled from Memphis with "a nephew and niece of Mr. Sneed." [27] An article in the *Tribune* of Henderson, North Carolina, discussed what a major event Miss Davis's visit was. Their "village," as the author wrote, due to its "remoteness from rail roads [*sic*], seldom [had] a peep at celebrities." The author went on to state that the congregation of St. John's Church was "on the qui vive" for

This lamp now hangs in the entry way of the Louise and Crawford Hill Mansion in Denver. It was once mistakenly reported that the lamp came from the house of Thomas Jefferson. After those who were in possession of the Hill Mansion consulted with individuals from Jefferson's house, they found that this was not the case. Rather, it is probable that the lamp (if of any notoriety) came from one of Jefferson Davis's homes, due to Louise Hill's familial relation to the Davis family. *Courtesy of Shelby Carr.*

Miss Davis, who they heard was in town to visit Major Sneed, though she did not attend church services.[28] Winnie was the youngest child of the Davis family and was born in the White House of the Confederacy in 1864; she later became known as the "Daughter of the Confederacy."[29]

Winnie's mother, Varina, the only first lady of the Confederacy, upon her death in 1906, was further linked with the Sneed family. An article in the *Rocky Mountain News* stated that Mrs. Davis, the "widow of the Confederacy" was actually a distant relative of Louise Sneed Hill. In the article, Hill gave an interview stating that Mrs. Davis was a "woman of a strong and dominant personality, the kindly and wholesoul [*sic*] hospitality, the genuine feeling of the typical Southerner with the vivacity and energy of the North." The article went on to state that Davis had just spent the summer season with Hill's sister in Canada, and though Davis was "slightly lame and always us[ed] a cane…[she] never tired of Mrs. Hill's two little sons, who were fond of her."[30] Supposedly, years later, Louise Hill—perhaps due to her familial connection to the Davises—came into the possession of a lamp that may have been from Jefferson Davis's home. She proudly displayed the lamp in the foyer of her Denver mansion.

CHILDHOOD

Louise Sneed Hill was reared, in her own words, in a "very puritanical family."[31] As a girl, she thought it dreadfully wicked to play cards and that it was one of the seven deadly sins for a woman to smoke.[32] Perhaps it was these early feelings of repression that fueled Hill, in her later years, to deem these actions not only acceptable in high society but standard and enjoyable.

During Louise's most formative years, at the height of the Civil War, her father—a lawyer by trade—served as the clerk of the county court (like his grandfather and other family members before him), and he served as a lieutenant in the Confederate army.[33] His sons, William Morgan and Richard G., also served in the Confederate army. The younger William, a second lieutenant in the Twelfth Regiment of North Carolina, was captured as a prisoner of war by the Union army in Spotsylvania, Virginia, on May 12, 1864, and he was jailed at the Fort Delaware Prison. Richard, a first lieutenant in the Forty-Fourth Regiment, was also listed as having been captured as a prisoner of war.[34]

All three Sneed men survived the war; the younger William and Richard eventually relocated to Memphis, Tennessee, while their father remained in North Carolina. The elder William Sneed married for a second time on March 14, 1866, to a local Granville County woman, Sarah "Sallie" Ann Lewis Bullock.[35] She was a widow and her first husband, James Madison Bullock, died under suspicious circumstances; citizens discovered his body slain on the side of a road in Granville. Bullock was a prominent member of the Granville community and owned the Aspen Lawn Plantation. The Aspen Lawn Mansion was, in the words of historian Samuel Thomas Peace, "an outstanding dwelling of its time."[36]

The *Raleigh North Carolina Semi-Weekly News*, on September 30, 1864, wrote about Bullock's death, stating that he was a "representative from the

Aspen Lawn Plantation was the home of James Madison Bullock and his wife, Sarah, before he was murdered. Seen here in 1955, Aspen Lawn was considered by local residents to be one of the most outstanding homes of its period. It has since been torn down. *Courtesy of the North Carolina Room, Granville County, North Carolina Library System.*

County of Granville in the legislature." He was reportedly found dead on the "old track of the Clarksville Railroad on the 28th, September. Cause of his death unknown." On October 9, 1864, the paper reported again that it appeared "James M Bullock, Esq....was murdered. He was shot through the head by some person unknown; his watch was missing and his money gone."[37] According to the history of Granville County, as relayed in Samuel Thomas Peace's work *Zeb's Black Baby*, Bullock was riding home on horseback from the town of Oxford on the day of his murder. Peace wrote that reports claimed Bullock "got to a little branch" about three miles from his home when he saw "the planks in the middle of the bridge were out of order." At that time, it was supposed that Bullock dismounted his horse to fix the planks and was shot.[38]

Rumors swirled through Granville that William Morgan Sneed was the murderer, because he was infatuated with Mrs. Bullock. Sneed was reportedly a very small individual, and at times, it was said that he would openly brag about how petite his feet were. Sneed apparently had custom boots made with an elevated heel in order to appear a bit larger in stature. Rumor has it that the heel prints of those custom boots were found around the slain body of James Bullock. Bullock's watch, which was mentioned as missing in the reports of his death, was a unique purchase that he made while traveling abroad. While it has never been confirmed whether or not he was actually wearing that watch at the time of his death, it could not be located after the murder.

The highly circulated rumor that has persisted through generations in the area tells the tale of Major Sneed owning a chest, or perhaps trunk, that he kept locked "in a little office in the yard." According to the tall tale, one day, Sneed had left the trunk unlocked, which resulted in a major discovery. He had supposedly been working on some of his accounts when he received an unexpected visitor at the gate—others claim a small fire broke out. In both of these instances, Sneed was distracted and left his valuable trunk unlocked. At that time, it is said that one of his servants, who appeared to either relay the message of the visitor or warn him of the fire, apparently viewed the missing Bullock watch in the open trunk. The servant then alerted Mrs. Sarah Sneed, who "verified the findings." After this discovery, the rumor mill produced the story that Sarah and two servants "soon died under mysterious circumstances."[39] The *Torchlight* newspaper reported on Sarah Sneed's death, stating in 1878 that she had "died suddenly" at the Aspen Lawn Mansion and that her "unexpected death le[ft] a blank in the social circle, in the church, and in her family, which will long remain unfilled. She was a model of the old-time, high-bred Southern lady—intelligent, refined, accomplished, and withal an [*sic*] humble, sincere Christian."[40]

A diary entry from the journal of Reverend William S. Pettigrew, on January 18, 1878, discussed the death of Sarah "Sallie" Sneed in detail. He wrote:

> *Friday at 4 p.m. left for Major Wm. M. Sneed, who had sent a conveyance for me. Arrived at his house 18 miles from Henderson, at 9 p.m. 17* [January] *Thursday, at 9:15 p.m. Mrs. Sallie A. Sneed, his wife died of apoplexy. She was first taken sick at supper on Wednesday night. Immediately after which she went to bed but was not sufficiently sick to require a physician. At 5 p.m. on Thursday, she had a spasm and was not conscious afterwards. She was 58. Her remains were carried to Williamsboro on Saturday. The funeral services were conducted in the church, and at 2 p.m., her remains were deposited in the grave.*[41]

Sarah Sneed was buried in St. John's churchyard beside William Morgan Sneed's first wife, Louisa "Louise" Maria Bethel, on Saturday, January 19, 1878. Due to the abrupt nature of her death, rumors swirled that Major

Sneed had poisoned his wife—a rumor that developed into a far-fetched idea that he had actually caused the death of both of his wives by poisoning them. It is highly unlikely that Sneed committed the murder of Bullock or poisoned his wives. He was never actually investigated by the authorities for any of these situations, but the rumor mill persisted. Most likely, the citizens of Granville were upset with Sneed for switching sides after the Civil War. He became a Republican after serving the Confederacy, and a lot of people saw him as a traitor for aligning with the ideals of their most hated enemy, President Lincoln. One account of the Bullock murder, as relayed by a Mrs. Blackburn, was published in the *Daily Dispatch* in September 1931; it discussed that Bullock was also an officer in the Confederate army and in the final days of the war had been tasked with arresting any soldiers he found deserting. Some have claimed that he was most likely shot by someone he caught deserting. Even generations later, Granville County citizens still pointed their fingers at Major Sneed for the crime. In 1931, Blackburn stated, "Within the year, he married the widow. This greatly shocked the community, and she was rather dropped by her former friends." Blackburn also said of Sneed that he was "the most handsome man with a gallant and charming manner and an engaging personality."[42] This information is a bit inaccurate. James Bullock died in September 1864, and Sneed did not marry his widow within the year; it was almost two years later, in March 1866, that the two were wed.

Nevertheless, William and the Sneed family remained prominent in the Granville community until his death. Diary entries from the Goodrich W. Marrow diary detail the events of Major Sneed's passing. Marrow wrote:

> *Wednesday, December 9, 1891—Sat up with Maj Sneed.*
> *Thursday, December 10, 1891—Maj Sneed died at 20 mins pas* [sic]
> *12 o'clock 1891. Mind perfectly clear to the last.*
> *Saturday, December 12, 1891—*[Major Sneed] *was buried at Wmsboro* [sic]. *I was paul* [sic] *bearer*[43]

The *Oxford Public Ledger* published on December 25, 1891, that "Major William Morgan Sneed…[one] of Vance county's most influential citizens, died."[44] He passed away at the age of seventy-two and was buried in St. John's Churchyard next to both of his wives on Saturday December 12, 1891.

Though Louise Sneed was baptized in North Carolina and lived with her father and stepmother for the early part of her life (an 1880 newspaper article lists "Miss Louise Sneed, North Carolina"), by the time of her father's passing, she had relocated to Memphis, Tennessee. The *Henderson Gold Leaf* published an article on December 10, 1891, that stated:

> *Miss Lou Bethell* [sic] *Sneed, a bright, charming and fascinating young lady, who has many friends and admirers in Henderson, has been stopping a few days with her sister Mrs. W.D. Burwell, in town. She was called from her home in Memphis, Tenn., by the announcement of a serious illness of her father, Maj. Wm. Sneed, at his residence near Townesville, for which place she left yesterday.*[45]

Though Louise was present at her father's home at the time of his passing, she was no longer a resident of North Carolina.

THE SNEEDS IN MEMPHIS

The exact years of Louise Sneed's residence in North Carolina and move to Memphis are not documented; in fact, Louise Sneed was never recorded in a single census in the states of North Carolina or Tennessee. The 1870 census listed her home and family members in North Carolina but did not include her. One interesting piece to note is that the 1880 United States census listed a "Louisa Sneed," who was aged seventeen years, born in North Carolina and living in New York City. This particular Louisa was also listed as a boarder who was attending St. Mary's School at 8 East Forty-Sixth Street; it is highly likely that this is indeed Louise Bethel Sneed. The 1915 publication *Woman's Who's Who of America: A Biographical Dictionary of Contemporary Women of the United States and Canada* by John William Leonard listed Louise Bethell [sic] Sneed Hill as the "dau. William Morgan and Louise (Bethell [sic]) Sneed; ed. N.Y. City."[46] Leonard's book and the 1880 census are the only sources still in existence that discuss her education in New York. St. Mary's was, in the words of *The Official Year-book of the Church of England* from 1886, "a boarding and day school for young ladies." A 1906 publication described the school as a college preparatory institution that also prepared young ladies for foreign travel.[47] According to the *Church of England* publication, there was an identical school in Memphis, Tennessee, which was also named St. Mary's School. Perhaps Miss Sneed spent a bit of time attending the New York location before choosing to relocate to Memphis to be closer to her family.

Louise Bethel Sneed, pictured here in her younger debutante years, was well known for her kindness. When the future Mrs. Hill was still Miss Sneed and lived in the South, newspapers noted that, when she attended dances, she "always singled out someone who wasn't popular, didn't have her dance and wasn't particularly attractive and tried to make it pleasant for her. She'd take men to her and introduce them and go out of her way to help the wallflowers enjoy the party. She was never afraid to entertain someone because other people didn't take them up, but that was sign enough for her to invite them." Columnists further noted that, due to her personality and kindness, "every man who ever knew her well proposed to her." *Courtesy of History Colorado, accession #90.314.328.*

Two of Louise's older brothers, William Morgan and Walter, moved to Memphis, Tennessee, in the 1870s, as reflected in both the city directories and the newspapers. The eldest Sneed child, William Morgan, was an attorney—he worked as Memphis's city attorney for two years—and he served as a partner at the prominent law firm of McRae, Myers and Sneed as early as 1873.[48] The later firm of Myers and Sneed also dabbled in the cattle business. Walter Sneed was living in Memphis by 1878, and he began operating a "clothing and gents furniture goods" store called Vendig and Sneed, according to the local city directory. Walter Sneed was also noted as a painter from Memphis in his October 28, 1888 wedding announcement in the *Inter Ocean*, a Chicago-based newspaper. Walter Sneed married Jessie Fenton of Illinois, and his sister, Louise, and brother, William Morgan, were both listed as residents of Memphis and as members of Walter's wedding party.[49]

Though the year that Louise Sneed moved to Memphis cannot be confirmed, it is highly likely her relocation occurred around 1884. The 1884 city directory for the City of Memphis listed a "Miss Louisa Sneed" living at the residence of 84 Court, the home of Louise's older brother, William M. Sneed of Myers and Sneed. One of Louise's elder sisters, Mary Bethel Sneed (regarded in newspapers as the recognized leader of Memphis's exclusive set for a time), and her husband, Hugh M. Neely, also lived in the city of Memphis alongside members of the Sneed siblings' biological mother's family, including their cousin William Decatur Bethel. Though she was not listed as a resident until 1884, Louise was already well known in the area and regarded as a member of the city's social scene. An August 16, 1881 article in the *Memphis Daily Appeal* stated that "Memphis [was] liberally represented" at the "charming mountain resort" of Mont Eagle Springs. The article went on to name Miss Louise Sneed as a "belle [there] as [she was] everywhere."[50]

The young Louise Sneed was a prolific feature in the society pages of Memphis's newspapers and made quite a name for herself within the upper echelons of the city's social circle. She was noted in the papers as one of the foremost belles of the South, and the *Richmond Dispatch* declared that she was the "belle *par excellence*" in 1886.[51] In the late 1880s and early 1890s, the Sneeds and Bethels of Memphis chose to build grand homes on Adams Avenue, which was then considered Millionaire's Row. Their section of the street also became known locally as the Sneed and Bethel Block.

THE CIVIL WAR IN THE SOUTH

While she was a highly desirable southern belle and wealthy debutante, the Civil War ravaged the area that the future Mrs. Hill called home. By delving into the context of what was happening in the world around her, we can better understand her future outlook and decisions based on the political climate of her youth. Prior to the commencement of the Civil War in 1861, the United States was a collection of institutions operating in conjunction with one another, but it was not necessarily a cohesive unit. As David M. Kennedy remarked in his editor's introduction to Richard White's *The Republic for Which It Stands*, before the war began "Americans commonly used the phrase 'the United States are.'"[52] This plural usage implied an existence of a collection of separate entities working together but not unified as a single nation. It was the hope of many northerners that at the end of the war, they would have one unified nation, under God (as later echoed by the Pledge of Allegiance, which was written in 1892 by Francis Bellamy). The Republicans dreamed of a free labor America in which equality reigned supreme and all families, regardless of their backgrounds, could attain a comfortable living in their chosen field; they also dreamed that upward mobility would once again be possible, just as it was in the fluid middle ground of the genteel class system of the earlier part of the century. In order for this vision of America to be achieved, Americans had to unify the broken pieces of the South and the vast, unregulated frontier of the West with the victorious, protestant, capitalist North. While individuals were attempting to manifest that reality, they were "unknowingly conceiv[ing] twins in 1865," and while the first twin "embodied the world they anticipated emerging from the Civil War…it died before being born."[53] The surviving twin lived on as the future of a new, United American country, and while, much like its deceased sibling, it "carried some of the noblest instincts and ambitions of the triumphant republic," it ended up bringing about some of the greatest disparities in wealth, class, violence and racial tension the nation had ever experienced.[54] Though the North did not first enter the war with the intention of abolishing slavery, by 1863, it was fighting for a "new birth of freedom," to redefine equality and what it meant to be American.[55] By the end of the war, the old America had passed away as "a casualty of the Civil War," and Americans sought to establish their visions of equality across the vast expanse of the United States.[56]

In the past, historians have drawn lines of demarcation to separate the Civil War, Reconstruction and the Gilded Age as three unique time periods. Defining a specific start and end date for Reconstruction and the Gilded

Age has proved challenging to various historians; while some place the commencement of the Gilded Age at 1870, others place it at 1877 (the most common end date for Reconstruction), and others still claim multiple alternative dates that coincide with the release of Mark Twain's novel *The Gilded Age*, which was the first source to provide the nomenclature of the opulent era.[57] The real issue here, as Richard White pointed out in *The Republic for Which It Stands*, is that historians define these periods as two separate, unattached entities by distinguishing a solid end of Reconstruction before the official start date of the Gilded Age. White suggests that the Gilded Age was not simply a product of reconstruction but rather had its roots in the earliest days of that era. White stated that "historians often write of Reconstruction and the Gilded Age as if they were separate and consecutive eras," when in reality, the "two gestated together."[58] The Gilded Age did not suddenly occur after the end of Reconstruction, but it gradually developed through the "splendid failure," as historian and civil rights activist W.E.B. Dubois penned, of the post–Civil War period.[59]

It was during this time that the American government received more power than it ever had before. As class lines began to become clearly defined, it was the emerging middle-class that saw a true need for increased government intervention in the post–Civil War era. It was the middle group and their crafted middle-class ideology that was perhaps the "greatest triumph and tragedy of Reconstruction."[60] While it was an "astonishingly inclusive way to run a country," it also "rendered Americans unable to recognize systematic inequalities in American society."[61] As the federal government began to intervene in reconstructing the nation and employ its "new powers" by "demand[ing] rapid and transformative change," it did not practice the idea of every man being equal under the new vision of the United States.[62] In the western part of the country, the "federal government boldly undertook policies considered too radical for the old Confederacy."[63] The government forced Native Americans to abandon the lands they had granted them in the West after driving them out of the eastern part of the country, and it took possession of the parcels and "redistributed them to both individuals and corporations," a process that had been rejected in the southern region of the country.[64] Actions such as these sparked an increase of hatred and violence. Though events such as the Sand Creek Massacre (the slaughtering of hundreds of peaceful Native Americans) occurred during the Civil War, the continued attacks on Native Americans, immigrants and African Americans after the war put the idea of equality and liberal individualism for all at risk.[65]

It was during this sensitive time of growing class disparity and race relations that technological advances and big business grew rapidly. America in the latter part of the nineteenth century became a place of "economic individualism."[66] Instead of striving for the Midwest dream of free labor equality that prevailed during Lincoln's reign, this later time period allowed for certain individuals to create empires and fortunes that had never before been seen in America. As Leon Fink noted in *The Long Gilded Age*, it was during this era that "mechanization took command and the autonomous conditions of craft control weakened," as skilled workers were replaced with cheap labor and machines.[67] This greatly denigrated the idea that all men could achieve equality in their chosen field of work. The former ideal of puritanical northern work ethic could no longer be achieved in a world of increased machinery and decreased skill. Instead, these developments pushed individuals into a state of poverty; before, those who lived in poverty were only those people who were unable to work not individuals who were physically capable of earning a living. As the wealth gap continued to grow between the working class and upper class, the middle-class Republicans "held firm to their free labor ideas, that every man could work his way up, self-sufficient and independent of government support."[68] This resulted in the groups of people who desired government aid to level the playing field—because of unfair treatment and the fact that they were forced out of their jobs—being "aggressively prohibited from participating equally in American society."[69] Perhaps unintentionally, subconsciously or unknowingly, middle-class Americans were actively working against their own idealist vision of America.

Throughout most of the literature concerning this time period there is a centralized theme that weaves through the narrative: the idea of the home as "the core institution of American society."[70] While this theme was prevalent at the time, the meaning of "home" was very different for the varying classes of post–Civil War America. As gender roles had to shift in the lower classes to accommodate for lost wages and deskilled labor, they were the first to see a different meaning to the traditional role that homes played in their everyday lives. As White noted, "[H]ome embodied all the gendered and racialized assumptions of American Republicanism and the American economy."[71] With the idea of a traditionally styled and gendered home environment at the core of the vision for the future of America, any perceived "threat" to that establishment—whether it be affluence, industrialization or urbanization—"became a threat to the entire society."[72] In the end, a huge point of contention during Reconstruction and the ensuing Gilded

Age was the struggle over class distinctions, and this conflict materialized at the end of the war and resulted in "a struggle over the home."[73] The idea of a standard home defining the nation was put into action by the attempt to make all of the varying geographic regions of America operate in the same capacity and emulate the "great" Midwest.[74] The Midwest was the "heartland" and, apparently, the "quintessential American place."[75] The idea that the virtuous people of the Midwest (with their hard work and small communities) were to be emulated in order to achieve this grand vision of post–Civil War America permeated the nation. When Abraham Lincoln was assassinated, the epitome of the Midwestern dream, the success story and the guiding leader of the future was gone. In their attempts to maintain the Republican dream, the American people ended up creating an entirely different country from the one they had set out to achieve.

Instead of achieving a vision of liberal individualism and equality, as Sean Dennis Cashman insinuated in his work *America in the Gilded Age*, the era rather exemplified the maxim "the ayes have it." Cashman felt this was ostensibly due to the nature of the era, which was dominated by self-importance (of "I") and spearheaded by the wealthy, who "rejoiced in the glitter of gold" and "define[d] many of the pervasive social themes" as opposed to the previous vision of a hardworking, individualistic America.[76] Between increased urbanization and federal government intervention in rebuilding the South and politically deriving and, over time, crafting the boundaries of the West (the arbitrary lines that Richard White asserted are "a series of walls pretending to be doors") in an attempt to create a unified nation, the individuals of the United States emerged from the Civil War with a country headed toward flourishing industry and wealth rather than a generalized middle ground.[77] American citizens, perhaps unknowingly, actively worked against their own desires for the country by continually denying those they deemed unfit the chance to better themselves. Mechanization made it almost impossible to achieve the elusive American dream, as the nation's once profitable industries and skilled apprenticeships began falling to the wayside in favor of cheap labor. Many of the authors previously cited touch on similar overarching themes: racial inequality, government intervention, deskilling labor, immigration, women's rights and class distinction. All of these issues can be attributed to the problems that developed in the post–Civil War Era. Unknowingly, American citizens helped create the factors they fought against as they attempted to implement the ideals of a free labor society with liberal individualism; all the while, the American market capitalist society continued to develop, flourish and create the Gilded Age.

LOOKING WEST

The Civil War devastated the population of marriageable young men with money in the South. The then-Miss Sneed, with her high ambitions, found that no one in the South had enough money to provide a vessel for her to achieve her ambitions. As she approached the age of thirty, the southern belle chose to expand her horizons, and she looked to the West for her future. The future Mrs. Hill had relatives who lived in territorial Colorado, and after stories of great wealth and fortune made their way eastward, from the Rocky Mountain region, she decided to leave the South and travel west to explore suitable marriage prospects.

A supposed sketch of a younger Miss Sneed, the belle par excellence of her time in the post-Reconstruction South. *Courtesy of History Colorado, accession #90.314.329.*

Hill chose to visit Denver, Colorado in 1893, and she stayed with her relatives Captain and Mrs. William D. Bethel. William Bethel had lived near Hill in Memphis in the 1880s and was her cousin on her mother's side; Bethel's father and Hill's mother were siblings.[78] Captain Bethel was a former officer in the Confederate army, and after moving westward, he became a prominent Colorado settler and financier.[79] He also served as the mayor of Memphis (or president of the taxing district, as Memphis had gone bankrupt during the Civil War and the state had repealed its charter), Tennessee, from 1891 to 1893.[80] Though Bethel served in Memphis during that time period, due to a physical breakdown in 1891, he moved his family to Denver, where he built a mansion at the intersection of East Colfax Avenue and Marion Street.[81] Perhaps word had traveled eastward of her cousin's successful business ventures in Colorado—Bethel had become the principal stockholder in the Southern Investment Company, and in 1891, he provided the financial backing for the Manhattan Beach Amusement Park on Sloan's Lake—as Louise Sneed blew into Denver like a whirlwind in 1893.

2

THE OLD GUARD AND THE CONTEMPORARY WOMAN

There was a small circle of wealthy individuals in Denver dubbed the "old guard" who preceded Hill's society group. It was at the height of the Gilded Age that the bold brunette made her first appearance in that meager, Denver social scene she came to revolutionize. The pioneer town possessed a limited circle of upper-class individuals, and upon arriving in Colorado, the then-Miss Sneed supposedly found it to be a "social wasteland," seemingly destitute of all the culture and customs she had been raised with. Denver was a town powered by the saloon and tavern business. In 1890, there were 478 saloons in the city, and many individuals felt the "absence of bars [was] a hallmark of a 'good neighborhood.'"[82] The presence of so many saloons meant that rowdy and, perhaps, uneducated patrons flocked to the city. Hill would have been confronted with a bit of culture shock and felt appalled at the lack of propriety and proper decorum in Denver.

Due to her cousin Bethel's prominence in Denver society and the early social scene, it was easy for Miss Sneed to make a proper entrance and attain introductions to Colorado's wealthiest families. Faced with finding a suitable husband upon her arrival, the "very beautiful and accomplished" Louise Sneed went to work scouring Denver for the perfect match.[83] She set her sights on the most eligible bachelor in town and the heir to the Hill family fortune, Crawford Hill. While it was said that "the heart and fortune of every eligible youth in town were laid at her feet," it was Mr. Crawford Hill—a successful businessman and son of Nathaniel P. Hill, the founder of Colorado's smelting industry, a U.S. senator and self-declared arbiter of Colorado society—who caught her eye.[84]

Crawford Hill, the son and heir to the wealthy mining magnate and U.S. senator Nathaniel P. Hill, was the most eligible bachelor in Denver in the 1880s and early 1890s. *Courtesy of History Colorado, accession #90.314.315.*

HISTORY OF THE HILL FAMILY

Crawford Hill was the first child and only son of the incredibly wealthy and prominent Nathaniel P. Hill (1832–1900); Nathaniel was "one of Colorado's outstanding pioneers."[85] Nathaniel was born into a distinguished family on February 18, 1832, in Montgomery, Orange County, New York. His great-grandfather Nathaniel Hill (around 1709–80) immigrated to the United States from Cavan, Ireland, around 1730.[86] He settled in a Scotch-Irish settlement in the mid–Hudson Valley region of upstate New York that is now known as the city of Montgomery in Orange County. Nathaniel came to America with wealth that he had previously amassed; his ancestors had possessed large estates in England and Ireland in the late sixteenth and seventeenth centuries. In 1768, he built a brick homestead and farm for his family in Montgomery, and the Hill family passed the property down through the generations. Today, it is a house museum.

Nathaniel's son, Peter (1751–95), Senator Hill's grandfather, became the sole owner of the brick home in 1779. Peter was a captain in the Revolutionary War, and at just twenty-four years old, he served in Colonel James Clinton's regiment of minute men.[87] Captain Peter Hill's son, Nathaniel P. Hill II (Senator Hill's father), took possession of the brick residence after his father's passing. Nathaniel was a prominent member of the community; he served as the sheriff of the town, was a "lieutenant of cavalry" in the War of 1812 and was a captain of the Orange Hussars (a local New York militia in Orange County).[88] He also served four terms in the New York general assembly, and from 1823 to 1825, he was a judge of the court of common pleas.[89] Nathaniel II and his wife, Matilda Crawford Hill, had seven children; Senator Nathaniel P. was their third.[90]

Nathaniel III was only ten years old and a student at Montgomery Academy when his father passed away. After his father's death, he continued his education while also helping his family run the farm.[91] He ran the family homestead until the age of twenty-one, when he decided to attend Brown University in Providence, Rhode Island. From an early age, the future senator had an interest in scientific agriculture, which led him to enroll in the chemistry program at Brown. He began his studies there with a "third-year standing" in 1854.[92]

Early in his studies, Brown's then-professor of chemistry, George I. Chace, greatly influenced Hill's success at the university. Chace's peers regarded him as "the ablest member of the faculty," who possessed a "remarkably clear, strong intellect."[93] In 1856, the year Hill graduated, Chace helped

Left: The Brick House, pictured here in 2018, was the childhood home of Nathaniel Peter Hill. *Courtesy of Shelby Carr.*

Right: Senator Nathaniel P. Hill, pictured here in his later years, revolutionized the mining industry in Colorado and established the first successful smelter in the western United States. *Courtesy of History Colorado, accession #90.314.306.*

Hill secure the position as his assistant. In 1858, Chace helped appoint him as instructor in chemistry applied to the arts. In 1859, Hill replaced Chace as the university's new professor of chemistry.[94] After his appointment, Hill set out to raise funds to build a brand-new chemical laboratory for his students. He succeeded in securing the funds for the lab's construction, and the structure was completed in 1862.[95]

In addition to teaching, Hill also dabbled in private consulting. He orchestrated various scientific inquiries for "local industrialists...analyzed autopsy materials for the city of Providence" and conducted an experiment concerning pollution in the Providence River.[96] At one point in his early career, Hill even took a leave of absence from the university to manage an oil refinery operation. Hill's work in chemistry at Brown, as well as his "integrity, thoroughness, and sound judgment," earned him a great reputation in the academic world as well as in high society and the business circles of Providence.[97]

While living in Providence, Hill met "a woman of superior powers and great sweetness of character," Alice Hale. Alice was born and raised in

Alice Hale Hill, pictured here in her later years, came from a prominent Providence, Rhode Island family. After marrying Nathaniel Hill and moving to Colorado, she was very involved with philanthropic organizations, including the founding of Denver's Free Kindergarten Association. *Courtesy of History Colorado, accession #90.314.303.*

Providence, Rhode Island, as a member of the prominent and prosperous Hale family.[98] Alice Hale was born the oldest of seven children on January 19, 1840, to Isaac Hale and Harriet Johnson Hale. The Hale family was prominent in the East, as they were descendants of Nathan Hale, a hero of the Revolutionary War. Alice's father, Isaac, was a watchmaker and jeweler by trade. Both of her parents had progressive views and were influential forces in the community. The Hales were very involved in the Baptist Church and actively supported female preachers. The Hales were also active, outspoken abolitionists, and Harriet Hale served as the recording secretary for the Providence Female Anti-Slavery Society in the 1840s.[99] Nathaniel and Alice were married in her hometown on July 26, 1860, and they had three children: Crawford (1862–1922), Isabel (1864–1926) and Gertrude (1869–1944).

Despite being of enlistment age during the Civil War, Nathaniel Hill never enlisted to fight for the Union. He had no ties to the Civil War other than his mandatory registration for the draft (President Lincoln signed the Enrollment Act into law in March 1863).[100] In 1863, Hill received two proposals from individuals seeking his assistance in investigations of mining properties;

The three Hill children,
Crawford, Isabel and Gertrude,
are pictured here in the 1800s.
*Courtesy of History Colorado,
accession #90.314.16.*

both of which he turned down. In 1864, Hill received correspondence from Colonel William Reynolds, a cotton and textile manufacturer from Providence. Reynolds wrote about a potential investigation of resources in the San Luis Valley of Colorado that he had invested in. He offered Hill a generous salary for his work—more than his yearly pay at Brown—to study (from April to December 1864) minerals present in the parcel of land he had invested in with former Colorado governor William Gilpin. Hill accepted Reynolds's offer and set out to reach the Colorado Territory by train and stagecoach. Once in Colorado, Hill visited Denver and Central City, in addition to the land encompassed in the Sangre de Cristo grant that Reynolds had employed him to examine. It is likely that Hill found no mineral value in the land, as after he submitted his report to Reynolds, the colonel sold his interest in the property.[101]

Hill's visit to the Colorado Territory sparked both his interest in the mining industry and his entrepreneurial spirit; he provided the executive board of the university with his resignation in November 1864 so that he could put his full attention into "practical metallurgy."[102] He had also purchased a house in Blackhawk prior to his return to Providence—an

The Nathaniel P. Hill family. *Courtesy of History Colorado, accession #2000.129.809.*

action that would appear to mean that he had an intention to return to the area, and he did just that.

Hill made two trips to the Rocky Mountain region in 1865 to study the complexity of removing precious metals from the deep recesses of the mines. He felt, based on the advice of a Welshman who was familiar with varying methods of recovering minerals from the earth, that there was a possibility of success in Colorado if they employed an alternative process of extraction to stamp milling (the most prevalent method in Colorado at the time). With the backing of Rhode Island investors, Hill arranged for a few tons of ore to be transported to the famous smelter in Swansea, Wales, that was responsible for the invention of the Swansea process.[103] Hill also traveled overseas in 1865 and 1866; he spent time studying metallurgy in Freiberg, Saxony, Germany, and researching the smelting process in Swansea, Wales, with the intention of constructing his own smelter in Colorado.[104]

Hill's shipment of Colorado ore was successfully processed by the Swansea smelter, and in 1867, he went about securing investors to establish a smelter in Colorado. He found support from easterners J. Warren Merrill, Joseph Sawyer, Gardner Colby and James W. Converse. The group of Boston businessmen invested $200,000 in Hill's business venture and named Hill "agent and local manager of the corporation" in the official paperwork the businessmen filed for their enterprise. They called it the Boston and Colorado Smelting Company.[105] Hill was regarded by many as "the chief agent in the creation of that great industry, which was necessary to the development of the mineral resources" of Colorado.[106] From "1868 to 1878, Hill's enterprise dominated the smelting industry in Colorado."[107] With the incorporation of the Boston and Colorado, Nathaniel Hill effectively established the first successful smelter and revolutionized the smelting industry in Colorado.

Hill and his family moved from Providence to Black Hawk, Colorado, in 1867 after the incorporation of the smelting company. At that time, he also acquired mining interests in Central City that saw great success. Due to his achievements and recognition within the community, Hill followed in his father's footsteps and went into politics. He was elected mayor of Black Hawk in 1871 and remained in that role until 1873. He also served as a member of the Colorado territorial legislature from 1872 to 1873. In 1879, three years after Colorado achieved statehood, he was elected (as a Republican) by the newly organized legislature to the United States Senate. He served in that role from March 4, 1879, until March 3, 1885, when he was defeated while up for reelection.[108] During his time in the senate, Hill

A group of workers at Nathaniel Hill's Boston and Colorado Argo Smelting Company standing around a stack of silver bullion bars. *Courtesy of History Colorado, accession #90.484.5.*

also served as chairman for the committee on mines and mining for the forty-seventh congress and sat on the committee for post office and post roads for the forty-eighth Congress.[109]

In 1879, Hill desired a more central location for his business and decided to move the Boston and Colorado from Black Hawk to the city of Denver. In "a classic move befitting the Gilded Age," Hill renamed the place Argo after the "mythical vessel…in search of the Golden Fleece" in Greek mythology.[110] Nathaniel and his business associates built the Argo smelter two miles north of the city of Denver, and it continued to thrive in its new location.[111]

While in Denver, Hill expanded his business interests. He engaged in the real estate business and aided in developing property around the capital city. In 1887, he helped form the Denargo Land Company and served as its president. His accomplishments continued to accrue; in 1891, he served as a member of the United States delegation to the International Money Commission.[112] He purchased a local newspaper, the *Denver Republican*, as well and served as president of the United Oil Company.[113] Some individuals also regarded him as the "originator of what will probably prove

Crawford Hill, looking dapper here, was a desirable prospect for marriage. *Courtesy of the Denver Public Library, Western History Collection, biography file folder Crawford Hill no. 2.*

to be the best plan for the establishment of the postal telegraph in this country."[114] During his time in England, Hill had studied postal telegraphy. While serving as a senator, he prepared a bill "well equipped with facts" and delivered a speech in the senate about his "exhaustive report" that would "probably be the basis for any future legislation on the subject."[115] Hill was one of the "gentlest, kindest, and most energetic of men," who, instead of "being a product of the Great West, the Great West [was] a product of him." He found great success in any industry he entered due to his remarkable work ethic, intelligence and prowess. Hill was not only a pioneer in the mining industry, the various other influential positions he held within the state of Colorado made him one of the most important and exceptional individuals in Colorado history. Nathaniel Hill helped shape early, pioneer Colorado, and he had a hand in influencing its development into the thriving state it is today. Upon his death in 1900, the *Weekly Courier* published the following:

> In the death of Hon. Nathaniel P Hill…the state loses one of its truest, best and most distinguished citizen[s], a man who has done more single-handed to promote the material welfare of the people and to advance the industries of Colorado than any other agency…served the nation with consummate skill and ability and reflected honor on the state and the people [he] represented. Colorado will long mourn the death of Nathaniel P. Hill.

While his father was the star of the show, Crawford Hill also held many well-respected positions—titles it appears he was able to gain in part due to his father's prominence. Hill was known as a capitalist and a banker. He was educated in the grammar schools of Blackhawk, Colorado, before going on to graduate from his father's alma mater, Brown University, in 1885. That same year, he began working for his father's newspaper, the *Denver Republican.* Following in his father's footsteps, Crawford also served as president of the Hill Land and Investment Company and the Denargo Land Company, and he was elected president of the board of trustees of his father's former business, the Boston and Colorado Smelting Company. His other positions included a stint as treasurer of the United Oil Company and Inland Oil Refining Company, second vice-president of the Associated Press, the director of the Mountain States Telephone and Telegraph Company, secretary of the Dolly Varden Mining Company and director of the Young Women's Christian Association (an organization that his mother was heavily involved in), the First National Bank of Denver and the Colorado Museum of Natural History. In 1900, he served as an alternate delegate for the state of Colorado for the Republican National Convention, and in 1908, he was chairman of the delegation for that year's convention.[116] The respect and wealth that came with the Hill name was attractive to Louise Sneed.

INTRODUCTION TO DENVER SOCIETY

When tiny but powerful Louise Bethel Sneed arrived in Denver in 1893, she made an immediate impact. The *Rocky Mountain News* announced on July 2, 1893, that "Mrs. H.M. Neely and her sister, Miss Sneed of Memphis," were visiting their cousin Captain Bethel and would remain in Colorado until the fall season. The article went on to praise Louise's appearance by stating she was a "beautiful and wealthy girl" and "a belle in the city where she resides."[117]

Various parties were thrown in honor of Miss Sneed's visit, including a small gathering on July 13, 1893, at Manhattan Beach. During her time in Denver, Hill's cousins Captain and Mrs. Bethel threw an opulent ball in her honor at their mansion on East Colfax, and they invited all of Denver's "society" of the time. Many of Denver's old guard society attended the black-tie affair, including the Moffats, Cheesmans and Hills. Crawford Hill, although rather devoid of a sparkling personality, made the acquaintance of the energetic Louise Sneed at that ball. It was the perfect match; what Crawford lacked in social presence, Louise more than made up for with her ambition, tenacity and drive to rule.

Louise Sneed returned to Denver in the summer of 1894, and on November 9 of that year, the couple announced their engagement in

Right: After her 1895 wedding, Louise Sneed Hill set out to revolutionize Denver's high society. *Courtesy of the Denver Public Library, Western History Collection, F22469.*

Below: The palatial residence of Captain William Bethel made a statement on the corner of East Colfax Avenue and Marion Street. *Courtesy of the Denver Public Library, Western History Collection, H-582.*

the *Denver Post*. Fourteen months later, the couple was married in a lavish ceremony in Memphis, Tennessee. The ceremony was conducted on January 15, 1895, at 8:00 p.m., and it was held at Calvary Episcopal Church. Calvary was founded in 1832, and the Sneeds began attending services there when they moved to Memphis. The church is located on Adams Avenue, just three blocks away from the mansions of the Sneed family that comprised the Sneed and Bethel Block. The opulent ceremony was covered in the society pages of newspapers all across the country. According to the *Times-Picayune* of New Orleans, Louisiana, the couple was wed by rector F.P. Davenport, and the "brilliant" reception was held at the home of Louise's sister, Mary Neely. The article went on to describe the wedding party in detail, stating that "the attendants were W.D. Bethel Jr. of Denver, best man, and Miss Hill of Denver, the bridegroom's sister, was maid of honor."[118] The *Omaha Daily Bee* published that Louise Sneed was a "belle of the south," and the wedding presents the couple received upon their union were "the most costly ever given in the South."[119]

In an article published in the *Aspen Daily Times* on January 16, 1895, titled "Crawford Hill Married," the author dubbed the bride, Miss Louise Sneed, "the reigning belle."[120] The *Denver Post* called the wedding a "fashionable" event that was attended by the elite of Memphis as well as the Denver citizens that Louise Sneed had fostered "warm friendships" with over her summer seasons with her cousins in the mile-high city. An article in the *Denver Republican* praised the new Mrs. Hill's beauty and her exquisite pearl white satin-and-chiffon gown, and it described the "superb diamonds" that sparkled "on her ensemble" that were a gift from Crawford.[121] In another untitled article, the Hill-Sneed wedding was described as a "beautiful, notable, and important event." The author described Mrs. Hill as "recognized everywhere as belle and a beauty," and they went on to further assert that "her marriage into a family as prominent as her own ma[de] it an occasion of unusual import and interest."[122] Just days after the wedding, on January 19, 1895, Hill's older brother, William Sneed, died of "softening of [the] brain."[123] Consequently, the *Denver Post* declared on February 1, 1895, that, though the newlyweds had arrived in Denver, most of the planned celebrations had been canceled.[124]

After their wedding, Mr. and Mrs. Crawford Hill established their home in Denver, and the new Mrs. Hill went to work building her empire. With Denver serving as her place of residence for the foreseeable future, Hill set off on a mission to reform the "social wasteland" that she supposedly deemed the mile-high city to be by establishing herself as it's leader and influencing culture and society to suit her ideals; but first, she had to tackle the established patriciate, the old guard.

Hill's new in-laws, Nathaniel P. and Alice Hale Hill, were members of this small group of Denver families who "had manners and charm" as well as "character and integrity," connections and money.[125] According to Marilyn Griggs Riley, Denver's old guard society served to "provide marriageable sons and daughters, to form corporations, to solidify water rights, to secure real estate investments…and shaped and ruled the city from Capitol Hill mansions."[126] Walter Cheesman and David Moffat (successful Denver businessmen who were among the original founders of the Denver City Water Company) were members of the old guard. These men believed that "what was good for them and their businesses was good for Denver and for Colorado."[127] They were very similar to the railroad tycoons at the time and those like them of the East. The old guard was an informal, small group but held incredible power over the city of Denver and its development from the water system to banking and other pertinent industries.

With their immense wealth and status in the Denver community, Senator and Mrs. Nathaniel P. Hill became arbiters of the old guard society. They owned a now-long-gone French chateau–style, twenty-room, three-story mansion at the corner of Fourteenth and Welton Streets, an area that early Denver citizens considered to be the city's first upper-crust neighborhood. Their wealthy neighbors included Governor and Mrs. John Evans, Mr. and Mrs. William Byers (the founder of the *Rocky Mountain News*), and Mr. and Mrs. John Wesley Iliff (the "cattle king" of Colorado). The old guard ran the city of Denver, its development and its politics, and the Hills were at the helm of the social scene.

The women of the old guard were of an older generation; they embodied the Victorian culture and stood as "a model of temperance, serving in a number of church, social and educational organizations."[128] Members of the old guard, such as Alice Hill, Margaret Evans and Elizabeth Byers, created societies like the Ladies Relief Society, the Denver Fortnightly Club (a study and discussion group organized in 1881), the Monday Literary Club and the Denver Orphans' Home.[129] These women established successful philanthropic societies but did not dare to stray too far from the norm of Victorian culture.

Alice Hill was a prominent force in philanthropy. In 1889, she signed papers to incorporate the Denver Free Kindergarten Association. The first meeting of the association was held at her home on October 23, 1889. The organization ultimately led to free early education for Colorado's children,

The Nathaniel P. Hill Mansion was an opulent residence on the corner of Fourteenth and Welton Streets, and it cost $40,000 to build. *Courtesy of the Denver Public Library, Western History Collection, Z-11786.*

and she served as its president for nine years. Also, in 1889, Hill began serving as the vice-regent of Colorado for the Mount Vernon Ladies' Association—a position she held until her death. As vice-regent, Hill was involved in the preservation efforts to repair and reconstruct George Washington's home. Having achieved her goals in organizing free education in the state, in 1893, Hill set her sights on propelling the women's suffrage movement. She helped circulate petitions throughout the state and was one of one hundred women who established the City League of Denver, an organization that was active in the women's suffrage movement and which she was a prominent force in. Hill's passion for female enfranchisement was shared with her children as well. Later that year, her daughter, Isabel, was one of the three young women who founded the Young Women's League in support of the same purpose. That same year, Alice Hill was a charter member of the Woman's Club of Denver. The organization maintained their headquarters at 1437 Glenarm Place and hosted suffrage events in their auditorium. Alice served as the president of the YWCA in Denver for eight years and was responsible for raising and donating most of the funds needed to purchase land, build a headquarters and furnish the building in the late 1890s and early 1900s. In 1900, Hill donated a gavel to the association; the gavel had been made from wood extracted from a magnolia tree planted by George Washington at Mount Vernon. Hill was also an active member of the Ladies' Relief Society and held events for the organization at her home in Denver. Alice Hill's accomplishments were meaningful and plentiful; though, aside from aiding in the 1893 campaign for women's suffrage, she did not stray far from the norms of Victorianism. Alice Hill and the other women of her circle were mainly involved in organizations outside the home that pertained to religion, preservation and philanthropy for those less fortunate. For the old guard, women in philanthropy were the epicenter of high society.

To Louise Hill, the old guard represented a high society of the past. She felt they were too stringent, and her ideas of luxury and gentility did not fit in with their vision of the upper crust. Hill also used the press, unlike her predecessors, to emphasize amusement and aid in her mission to transform society from Victorian morality to unabashed fun. In 1908, a newspaper article in the *Denver Post* published a story of Hill's roller-skating escapades. The article stated that Hill was roller-skating around the ballroom of her home

In 1889, Alice Hill began serving as the vice-regent of Colorado for the Mount Vernon Ladies' Association, a position she held until her death. She played a role in preserving the structure. Alice and N.P. Hill were captured here by the Mount Vernon official photographer on one of their visits. *Courtesy of History Colorado, accession #90.314.309.*

LAWN FETE GIVEN BY MRS. CRAWFORD HILL

A large group of attendees are pictured here at a lawn fete given by Louise Hill at her home for the Belgian Babies Fund in conjunction with the Junior League. *Courtesy of the Denver Public Library, Western History Collection, Z-1023.*

when she, unfortunately, broke her wrist.[130] Instead of acting as a Victorian reformer, Hill sought to loosen the reins of the elite and emphasized lively, amusing activities of a modern era. When asked by a newspaper reporter how she intended to go about reforming fashionable society, Hill replied: "Reform fashionable society? Good gracious! It doesn't need reforming. If anything, it's too particular. It is becoming so strict that, soon, one will need to undergo something like a eugenic test to qualify for it."

Unlike the women of the Victorian old guard, Louise Hill felt that charitable contributions were no longer the sole role of a genteel woman or the only suitable activity for them outside the home. In another contradictory aspect of Hill's life, there was one topic that she claimed she chose to keep out of the newspapers: her charitable contributions. Hill stated in an interview with the *Rocky Mountain News* in 1913 that she "would rather give [her] dances to the papers than [her] charities." She said, "It is better to advertise your dinners and your luncheons, so-called frivolous things, than to advertise your charities, which touch something sacred—humanity—and which reach into our religion—Christianity." The author of the article went on to state that though Mrs. Hill "refuse[d] to discuss her charities…[she] happen[ed] to know they [were] many and efficacious despite the fact that they do not head the lists flaming in the garish lights of publicity." Hill did not believe in "heading lists with [her] name and getting into spectacular advertising in the name of charity," but she hoped that she did her part in aiding those who could not help themselves.[131]

...IDENCE FOR THE BELGIAN BABIES FUND

One charitable act that Hill could not keep from the newspapers was her support of the American troops during World War I. She frequently donated her time and funds to the cause. When the war broke out, she took it upon herself to help. She created and served as the director general of the soldiers' family fund and called for all Coloradans to donate their support to the cause. The people of Colorado answered her plea, and the fund saw donations as high as $2,000 a day at the height of the conflict. She was dedicated to her state and to the country. When asked about the outpouring of support she received for her fund, Hill said:

> *I am proud of the way Colorado is responding....I'm proud and happy to know that patriotism glows so strongly in the hearts of Coloradans. While I've always prayed for peace, I believe that first and last and always the honor of this country should be maintained. I'm going to try to do my share. It isn't a Denver proposition, it belongs to all of Colorado.*[132]

Hill did so much for the cause that an ambulance serving the American troops in France was named after her. Ambulance number 1030 bore the inscription "Mrs. Crawford Hill, Denver, Colorado, U.S.A.," and it served one of the stations where the American field service in France was serving with the French army at the front.[133] It appears that, while Hill felt that philanthropy was an essential part of being a good Christian and human being, it did not have a place in high society. She differed from the old guard in defining a genteel woman as one who acted charitably publicly. Instead, she chose to keep her philanthropic efforts out of the public eye, as it was not an integral aspect of her social game; charity was not to be competitive and did not help an individual win recognition in Hill's high society contest.

While Hill's motives for transforming Denver's high society were never clearly stated in her own words, it seems through her actions that she had a complex compilation of desires. She wanted to provide a grand society for the residents of Colorado and give back to the community in terms of cultural relevance on an international scale. She also wanted to put herself in the spotlight and modernize the formerly strict Victorian ideals of the genteel woman. The existence of the old guard, regardless of its Victorian morals and standards, gave Louise Hill a solid foundation to transform Denver's high society and was a perfect legacy for her to inherit from her in-laws. While she had her own ideas of breathing life back into the restrictive society she felt the old guard to be, Hill looked to the East for notions of how to take her objectives and elevate her revolutionized society to a recognized modern beau monde on a national and, eventually, international scale.

IT HAPPENED ON FIFTH AVENUE

The Gilded Age, an era of decadence in the United States, is still known today as perhaps the most lavish period in the country's history. Money was key and appeared to rule all. Modest, unassuming dress and decorative style was out of fashion, and the more apparent you could display your great wealth through opulent parties and expensive objects the better. There was nowhere in which opulence, high society and class division were more apparent than they were in New York City.

The formation of the bourgeoisie in New York began centuries before it came to full fruition during the Gilded Age. Families such as the Astors, Beekmans, Schermerhorns, Van Burens, Van Rensselaers, and Whitneys settled in New York during and prior to the eighteenth century and had made somewhat of a name for themselves. They were predominantly Dutch settlers and were known as the Knickerbockers, so named after the knee-length pants that were worn by the Dutch. According to historians Gail MacColl and Carol Wallace, Knickerbocker families were typically landowners, heirs, lawyers and bankers who lived in modesty in side-by-side brownstones, hosted sophisticated events, and dressed with a moderate refinement and practicality.[134] Some knickerbocker men involved themselves in big business and continued to grow their family fortunes during the late nineteenth century. The Knickerbocker society developed into the aristocracy of "old" New York during the Gilded Age. They ran the press in New York City and heavily controlled what newspaper reporters said about them and others in their social spectrum. This helped them effectively create their class exclusivity. Therefore, they were able to create a public persona in which they were the epitome of high class and unattainable but forever desired success.

New York City was a thriving metropolis, and by 1800, it was the largest city in America. As the country's cultural and social capital, the city continued to flourish during the Gilded Age. New York City, which had once held a small population of thirty thousand at the turn of the nineteenth century, roughly doubled in size every decade henceforth. This rapid increase in population resulted in approximately 4 million people residing within the city limits by the beginning of the twentieth century.[135]

New York also became the hub for two-thirds of the United States' imports and one-third of its exports by 1860, due to the rise of industry that occurred there. New York developed as the polestar for American manufacturing operations and the financial and commodities markets. It also became the home to Wall Street, banks and various insurance companies; it developed into a wellspring of funds for the United States, and as Beckert wrote, "its wealth dwarfed that of all but London and Paris."[136] New York City soared to new heights of artistic sophistication during the Gilded Age as well. According to historians such as Sean Cashman, because of innovations in art, literature and architecture, the Gilded Age also became known as the "American Renaissance," a term coined by F.O. Matthiessen.[137]

New York—as the metropolitan hub for big business, great wealth and cultural richness—quickly developed into the location to be for high society folks, and "all American society [was] modeled on that of New York," because what occurred there had consequence.[138] Throughout the Gilded Age, the New York elites (both old money and new money) continued to garner and possess most of the nation's wealth and became increasingly public in displaying their fortunes. This was due in part to the conflict within the upper class. Many of the new money families—mostly those who had earned their wealth through the stock market or through becoming tycoons in the big business world—chose to settle within Manhattan's borders and started building grandiose mansions along Fifth Avenue, right across from many of the old money families' modest-looking brownstones. For the queen of the social scene, Caroline Astor, their actions were unacceptable. When a bold nouveau riche man, Alexander Turney Stewart, dared to use his fortune to build a mansion of, as author Eric Homberger stated, "broad-ranging vulgarity" right across the street from Astor's own home, she fought back with a vengeance.[139] In 1893, Astor arranged for a new mansion to be built for her family and intended for it to be most opulent, far surpassing any home occupied by arrivistes, and she made sure that it included a magnificent new ballroom.

LOUISE HILL LOOKS TO THE EAST

Louise Hill, when forming her Sacred 36 society in Denver, followed the example set by Mrs. Caroline Astor's New York Knickerbocker society. Astor crafted an aristocratic-style society in New York City in which money, lineage and prestigious titles gained acceptance and entrance. Astor developed an exclusive list of four hundred names of the individuals who fit her specific criteria, and they were allowed entrance into the elite society of New York City. Astor ruled New York and defined it as the center of high society social life in the country. Historian Dixon Wecter defined Astor as "the social leader of greatest fame and most undisputed authority in the history of the United States."[140]

Scholars have generally attributed the emergence of this particular New York society to the sudden appearance of the nouveau riche. Eric Homberger stated in his work *Mrs. Astor's New York* that it was the eruption of all of the new wealth in New York City after the Civil War that "pushed the city's old families into a redefinition of the practices and responsibilities of aristocracy."[141] This redefinition was necessary because the New York elites were "living in a community undergoing rapid social change, in which older values, taste, decorum, and social standards were dissolving." This rapid change ultimately pushed the old families to yearn for a society like the four hundred.[142] It was Astor who defined the customs of the emerging bourgeoisie and helped to take America's aristocracy from "a metaphor for high social status or prestige" to that of a recognized, self-defined actuality for a small subset of families in upper-class New York.[143] Other historians have argued that the bourgeoisie came to fruition during the Gilded Age because culture suddenly permitted women to enter a more public sphere and create the society—because society is inherently feminine.

Dixon Wecter's work *The Saga of American Society a Record of Social Aspiration*, which was originally published in 1937, was an in-depth look at high society, the social elite and their antics. Wecter was perhaps the first historian—and the only one for decades—to attribute the creation of high society partially to the women as well as the men (if only in just one short chapter of his 483-page work). Wecter penned that, in every time period "where women have been given relief from labor and an honorable place, society has bloomed."[144] He felt this was the case because "society is feminine," ranking "strategy above directness," and that women, as "custodian[s] of the cultural as well as the physical germ-plasm…[have] an instinctive appreciation of the codes, barriers, patterns, and traditions which the formation of social classes creates."[145] As Emily Bibby asserted, while the men had economic capital, the women maintained cultural capital.[146] The cultural capital and the influence of those women was just as integral a part of establishing the bourgeoisie as the men's economic work.

DEVELOPING CLASS CONSCIOUSNESS

Where there is money, there is conflict, and the upper echelons of society felt this struggle greatly during the Gilded Age. Not only did those of old money (the New York Knickerbockers) take issue with those of new money (the nouveau riche), but because of the massive wealth attained during this time, there was a great divide between the "haves" and the "have-nots." Conflict was created between classes and within classes. Harsh judgments were imposed on many—if not all—members of society, as the unspoken requirements of a mold that all individuals had to fit were strictly adhered to. Astor and others within the upper echelons of society, wielded a power to impose these judgments on individuals. As Homberger stated in his book *Mrs. Astor's New York*:

> *The judgement made by Mrs. Astor and other society leaders upon who was socially acceptable was erected on a complex system of regulations, informal controls, and social rituals which sought…to impose constraints. The aim behind such acts of exclusion was the set standards of behavior in public and private places, as well as establishing appropriate dress, forms of entertainment, domestic décor, and dozens of other aspects of the daily lives of those who were in society, and those who hoped to secure their admission.*[147]

Many of these specifications for bourgeois behavior were also derived from etiquette books. Courtesy and conduct books, a precursor to the etiquette books of the nineteenth century, arrived in America in the eighteenth century and served as a tool to instruct young women and men on how to behave properly in social settings. These books set the rules for gentility in the United States.[148] Nowhere were these rules more recognizable than in New York City, where Astor ruled with the power "bestowed upon her by others expressing a collective judgement upon Mrs. Astor and what she represented."[149] Astor formed her society to maintain control on polite society, and she clearly set the class boundaries.

The formation of class identity was prevalent during the Gilded Age. While in prior decades, it was an unspoken norm, a class structured society came firmly into popular consciousness in the late nineteenth century. For centuries, women were viewed as subservient to men; they were deemed to be the weaker sex by early philosophers, considered unable to meet the same physical demands or produce intelligent thought equal to that of men. A woman's nature was considered to be "determined by the sexual and reproductive organs of the lower body. When the constraints of morality or self-control were…relaxed, women reverted to a state of biological and sexual anarchy."[150] In other words, women could not be in control of their own place in society when they could not even control themselves. When beliefs such as those were prevalent, society was male-driven, as men were the only ones permitted to enter the public sphere—women remained entirely in the private sphere. Men ran society, and class lines were not drawn in definite layers but were rather viewed as a fluid chain, from the lowest of laborers to the highest of genteel manhood. As traditional views on gender began to change over the course of the nineteenth century, and as Victorian culture came and went, women began defining their power by entering the public domain, both socially and in the workforce. These shifts in gender constructs consequently guided class identities through a gradual progression, from a fluid middle ground, to (by the mid-nineteenth century) the development of defined, separate class consciousness and finally, by the time the Gilded Age had fully blossomed, to the public recognition of three distinctly defined class identities, each with their own qualities, definitions and methods of enforcement and regulation. These three periods of class consciousness culminated in perhaps the most critical period of class development in American history, the Gilded Age.

At the beginning of the nineteenth century, the heroes and figures of the Revolutionary War began to fade away. While those individuals championed the separation from the aristocratic values of England, nineteenth-century Americans began looking back to Europe for social and cultural cues as they continued to develop American society.[151] Americans clung tightly to the idea of gentility and polite society as their capitalist society continued to grow and thrive. As Richard Bushman stated in his work *The Refinement of America*, "capitalism and gentility were allies in forming the modern economy."[152] The American version of gentility, however, provided space for growth, as a large middling ground was developing that would serve as a fluid space for individuals to pass through on their way to achieving status within their communities. This style of gentility differed from its European origins in two capacities. First, it lessened the divide between a formalized gentry class and the rest of society by moving it to "a lower level and separated the middle class from workers and marginal people."[153] Second, this genre of gentility "offered the hope that anyone, however poor or however undignified their work, could become middle-class by disciplining themselves and adopting a few outward forms of genteel living."[154] The broadly defined middle class of the early nineteenth century consisted of "smaller merchants and professionals, ordinary well-off farmers, successful artisans, schoolteachers, minor government officials, clerks, shopkeepers, industrial entrepreneurs and managers."[155] Men were urged to practice the behaviors of a genteel gentleman, as "gentility bestowed social power," and males maintained the class status that defined their families while women were confined to the home and tasked with maintaining a proper, genteel household.[156]

While poverty was not prevalent in America at the time, with the turn of the nineteenth century, labor began its earliest stages of alteration, and many laboring men faced the challenge of being able to support their families. This insufficiency in being able to provide sparked a change in the male-female relationships of the working class. As time progressed, the laboring class increased its numbers, as "urban migration and the beginnings of urban manufacturing spelled the disintegration of the customary household economies that had formerly absorbed the energies and loyalties of women."[157] While men had previously acted as the providers, with women managing household duties, this dynamic shifted, and men lost the authority that they had become "accustomed [to] within their households and workplaces."[158]

The nineteenth century's early distinction between the lower and broad middle classes was not a major issue for American society. As Bushman argued, the "marginalization" of the lower class "did not intensify class consciousness among the lower orders" at the time.[159] The issues of a thoroughly defined class system were not publicly acknowledged or fully realized until the Gilded age. As Bushman said, "The spread of gentility confused rather than clarified the issue of class," and it was not until the intense wealth disparity of the Gilded Age and the emergence of females in society—policing it with their assertion and maintenance of cultural capital—that the three-class system became distinctly defined.[160]

As the nineteenth century progressed, class identity began to shift as gender roles were altered within the home. These changes not only occurred in the working class; in the middle of the nineteenth century, a more defined middle-class consciousness began to emerge, and they saw shifts in gender roles as well. Where once men were in charge of family dwellings, that power began to shift as women started exercising control in the private sphere that they had been previously been confined to. Stansell argued in her work *City of Women* that women began exerting power in their households, as they felt their residences to be "the sphere of society where they could most effectively" employ such authority.[161] This confinement, Stansell argued, caused women to suffer "constriction of their social engagements"; however, "they gained power within their families that also vested them with greater moral authority in their communities."[162] This description of Victorian culture reigned supreme during the mid-nineteenth century and defined how women could articulate their class identities.

Victorian culture was driven by censuring pleasures, women remaining in the home and work ethic. Women in Victorian culture were to be the "moral guardians" of their husbands and children; "they appropriated the role of guardians in society."[163] With that great responsibility, women were unable to partake in many social pleasures outside the home for risk of being deemed fallen women and ruining the reputations of their families. As women embraced these requirements, a middle class began to find its definition.

Part of the role of respectable Victorian women was to serve their communities by partaking in charitable work through their local churches and institutions designed to give back to the less fortunate. As these women increasingly made these tasks pertinent pieces of their identities in society, a rift was created between the middle-class women and those who led a working-class life. The fluid middle class of the prior decades, in which anyone could attain middle-class status through hard work, became increasingly more difficult to enter, as middle-class women "refined their own sense of themselves as social and spiritual superiors" to those who needed to work for a living.[164] As Stansell wrote, "domesticity quickly became an element of bourgeois self-consciousness."[165] As more vices began entering the social scene (gambling, burlesque, risqué theater, drinking, frivolous dancing, et cetera) the middle class began to separate itself from the working class and minorities who engaged in such behaviors. As Robert Allen stated in his work *Horrible Prettiness*, "the creation of the bourgeois self was predicated on the exclusion of the popular as that which was not respectable, tasteful, or clean."[166]

While the middle class began finding its identity, skilled laborers began to evaporate in the face of increasing industry, and many former craftsmen in the middling class of the earlier part of the century found no place for themselves in this burgeoning class system of the mid-century.[167] While they had previously been able to reside in the flexible middle, "by the middle of the nineteenth century, vernacular gentility had become the possession of the American middle class."[168] These "middling groups," according to historian Alan Trachtenberg, "took their cultural bearings from their own insecurities in the changing world."[169] The influx of unskilled labor immigration and the rise of big business—especially that of the manufacturing industry—left little room for a successful, skilled laborer and further isolated individuals from the potential to climb the social ladder.[170] It was during the mid-nineteenth century that the former apprenticeship society disappeared in favor of wage labor, and learned skill fell to the wayside of cheap, unskilled labor.[171] These developments in American society ushered in the distinct class divides of the latter half of the nineteenth century.

Disparity in wealth hit an all-time high during the Gilded Age, as it became an era dominated by the wealthy citizens of America. As certain families made fortunes that cemented their high-class statuses, others fell to the lower ranks, and by the 1870s, the wealthy had "articulated a consciousness of separate class identity" due to the emerging middle class.[172] While an elite, upper-class existed prior to the Gilded Age, it was not until the end of the Civil War that this class asserted its power and began policing its bounds, defining strict lines that did not allow for upward mobility. The men of the Gilded Age channeled the power they had lost in the home in previous decades and focused it toward building America's various industries. Those men of the upper class became known as the "robber barons," or those individuals who maintained the economic side of society and class distinction, while the women of high society entered the public sphere through managing cultural and social functions. The Civil War brought about the ideas of Westward expansion and of securing fortunes, achieving the "American Dream" and accomplishing the ultimate destiny of the time: becoming the high-ranking self-made man—the idyllic rags to riches story.

The period between the late nineteenth and early twentieth centuries was also a time when mass consumption began to take root. With the invention of movies, the creation of celebrity culture and the popularity of displaying wealth through ostentatious belongings and dwellings, this time in American history was lavish, and every American citizen became painfully aware of their place in society. Women were no longer required to abide by the Victorian culture standards of remaining only in the home or in participating in charitable acts while they were in public. At this time, class lines were quite frequently defined by material possessions, as women were tasked with defining social class and men with economic class.[173] These clearly defined class boundaries created an impassable gulf between the haves and have-nots and brought about some of the greatest periods of turmoil in American history, as the working class found itself in a position with no hope for improvement, and the middle class sought to emulate the upper echelons; all the while, those of the upper class made every effort to increase the exclusivity of their ranks.

As Allen stated in *Horrible Prettiness*, "power is expressed through ordination…[regulating] through the arrangement of things in ranks and orders—what is high, what is low; what is us, what is them."[174] This fact was never more apparent than it was in the early years of the twentieth century. Americans, especially those of the upper classes, sought to further define the classes by creating stratifications within them; the middling group was further divided into three sections that included the lower, middle and upper middle classes, while the upper class used the distinction of nouveau riche and old money to demarcate the differences between those ostentatious folks who had recently garnered their fortunes and those who had possessed wealth for decades and centuries prior.

As time moved forward, the culture of consumption continued to alter these class lines further by allowing those of different classes to have shared experiences (like those they had in movie theaters).[175] In later decades, the importance of class distinctions began to fade, as ethnic and racial lines took center stage and those whites of the laboring class began to identify with their middle and upper-class employers rather than their peers due to ethnic differences.[176] Between 1800 and 1917, society saw great evolution in gender roles that defined the class system of the time and made the period recognizable as that of the emergence of the middle class and the first publicly recognized system of class consciousness, and it served as an era of great division between members of the same nation based purely on economic circumstance.

Gilded Age Identities—East and West

The beginning of the Gilded Age signaled a shift in society in various capacities. Many Americans became obsessed with the idea of attaining great wealth and doing whatever it took to earn fortunes for themselves. It was a society consumed with industrialization, invention and incorporation.[177]

The surge of new industry and the rise of big business that occurred in America during the Gilded Age created an "impassable gulf" between those who were considered to be of a dependent class, or working class, and those who were upper class (those who owned the various institutions and garnered great wealth). It created a large rift between individuals, even those residing in the same communities; at one time, they shared some common experiences, but they no longer could relate to each other. As the working class fell further down the economic ladder, aligning itself more with urban communities and those of various ethnicities, the upper class defined its own type of aristocratic rule and developed new cultural norms all its own.[178] While Hill looked east, to Mrs. Astor to find inspiration for her social norms, New York society had turned further east and hearkened back toward the cultural cues of European aristocracy.

The analysis of a publicly conscious class identification system served as one of Sven Beckert's main points in his work *The Monied Metropolis*. Beckert asserted that, in comparison to the British bourgeoisie, which "had already developed a sense of shared identity" earlier in the century due to prior conflict, the American bourgeoisie developed apropos to the establishment of the working and middle classes.[179] He continued his argument by asserting that it was the desire of the New York City's bourgeoisie to "assimilate the cultural norms of the European ruling classes of past centuries" that contributed to their successful creation of an American aristocracy.[180] In Beckert's words, their actions "expressed the enormous confidence, power, and wealth of upper-class New Yorkers."[181] In essence, it was the recognition of that system that allowed the bourgeoisie to not only establish their assumed superiority but to perpetuate it as well.

Historians Carol Wallace and Gail MacColl focused on class identity in the Gilded Age and compared British aristocracy with the American bourgeoisie in their book *To Marry an English Lord*. In opposition to British aristocracy, which was rooted in the foundation of centuries of ancestry, MacColl and Wallace felt that the American aristocracy was built on foundations of money.[182] During the Gilded Age, a specific distinction arose between the nouveau riche and the old aristocracy. Due to this classification within the upper-class social identity, a number of newly wealthy, young American women traveled overseas to marry gentlemen of British peerage. As MacColl and Wallace stated, the "crucial question" in New York City high society was "whether or not Mrs. Astor 'knew' you. Had she spoken to you at a tea party? Had she paid you a call?"[183] The most important question, the authors wrote, was whether or not Astor had extended you an invitation to her annual ball. If she had not, "you'd best leave town or sit at home in the dark lest anyone know of your shame."[184]

While the divide between the working class and upper class was obvious to even the most untrained eye, the distinction between old money and new money families within the same social class was not necessarily apparent to those outside of its circle. This blurry distinction was not confined to the larger cities, such as New York; Denver felt its effects and prejudices as well.

After Astor's exclusive club came into the limelight, other cities attempted to follow suit. Newport, Rhode Island, had a society they dubbed the Mighty Ninety, which included many influential individuals from Washington, D.C., as well as some from New York City, who had built palatial summer homes in the summer haven.[185] Cities in the eastern part of the country, like New York and Newport, were of an older generation of establishment. They had been in existence for over a century before the Colorado Territory became a state. Colorado, unlike the states of the eastern coastline, was not an epicenter for big business during the early years of the Gilded Age. The city of Denver in the Colorado Territory, which became a state in 1876, varied greatly from other American cities in terms of geographic landscape, successful industry and population. Astor had many "old money" families to choose from when deciding on who to include in her 400, while Louise Hill had a much smaller population of long-standing wealth to work with.

While Astor's model for elite societal success laid the framework for Hill to establish Denver's high society, Hill had many other factors to consider. First, Louise Hill had a different definition of gentility from both Caroline Astor and Denver's old guard. Where Astor and the old guard relied more on conservatism, Hill had a somewhat more modern vision for society. Hill was a member of a younger generation, a transitional generation. If she had been born a generation earlier, it is reasonable to assume that her ideals would have aligned with Astor and the old guard, who were consistently focused on Victorian gentility. If she had come into the world a generation later, she likely would have been a flapper, a character straight out of *The Great Gatsby*. While Hill looked to Astor as a model of ultimate societal success—and employed some of Astor's tactics, such as the idea of society taking the form of a club membership or a tightly policed social circle—she utilized them differently.

Hill, at times, publicly separated herself from the ideals of Astor in order to establish her own societal identity. While she sought to be Astor's western equivalent, it was important for Hill to be recognized on her own accord. In an interview with Alice Rohe of the *Rocky Mountain News*, which was printed in a 1913 article, entitled "Society as Fine Art," Hill specifically disregarded the notion that she embodied the exact same ideas of genteel womanhood (in terms of serving as a society leader) that Astor had. Rohe asked Hill if she agreed "with the statement of a well-known magazine writer that a social leader must have an indomitable will and must always hold herself aloof and on a slightly higher plane than her followers." Hill replied with a laugh and stated, "That may [have been] descriptive of Mrs. William Astor, but, understand…society to me means the opportunity of being with congenial people who I am fond. A social leader must be kindhearted and considerate and gently bred."[186] Hill wanted to be regarded as more relatable, modern and open in her thinking and policing of society. She sought to be recognized as her own version of a society leader based on her more modern thoughts.

A second issue for Hill when forming her society was geographic location. Colorado's industries and migratory patterns were vastly different than those of New York. At the end of the Civil War, the western portion of America was looked on as a "region of inexhaustible resources, where labor could easily realize profit from nature."[187] The climate of Colorado was believed to be a dream for the agricultural industry and those interested in ranching and similar disciplines. In essence, it was hardly a population of glitterati.

While Colorado became a state on August 1, 1876, its life did not begin that day, and its pre-statehood past was not erased. In prior decades, there was a common misconception that the American West was a barren, dark land ripe for the taking by those individuals who were brave enough to embark on their dream of traveling west and starting a new life on the final frontier. This idealistic vision of the American West attracted individuals, such as Lewis and Clark, to explore its soil, and events like the gold rush brought masses of people to the Rocky Mountain region in search of earning their fortunes and living the American dream. Contrary to popular belief, as historian Elliot West stated in his work *The Contested Plains*, the "Comanches, Kiowas, Cheyennes, Lakotas, and Arapahoes did not move in to a place empty of history" when they inhabited the territory that would come to be known as Colorado, just as white settlers did not "march into a storyless land" when they decided to venture westward; rather, the "plains have some of the oldest, richest history in North America."[188]

The Pikes Peak gold rush (1858–61) was perhaps the main instigator for westward migration to Colorado in the nineteenth century. There were various stories that spread across the country concerning the gold territory, and they all promoted large findings of mineral deposits and encouraged individuals to travel to the Rocky Mountains in search of making a fortune.

Pieces like "Our Central Gold Region—The Pike's Peak Mining District," which was first published in the *New York Herald* and again in the *Rocky Mountain News* on September 7, 1860, stated, "The Pike's Peak district may therefore be henceforth regarded as one of the gold producing regions of the world."[189] It was due to these types of reports that the gold-seeking spirit was kept alive across the country, and westward migration remained popular into the 1890s. The popularity of mining and agriculture spawned a large contingent of poor, working-class individuals who were hoping to make fortunes through hard labor. The mining industry was huge in Colorado, and while there were successful prospectors, investors and others who became wealthy mining magnates, there were also poor individuals who worked in the mines, and as Thomas Andrews mentions in his work *Killing for Coal*, these workers were sometimes considered to be "an inferior class of beings."[190]

In Denver, there were far more working-class and middle-class individuals than there were members of the leisured class. In the city's early days, there was no substantial upper class to be found, only the old guard, who occupied a minute section of the city. The mining industry did give way, however, to other successful industries out of necessity and helped create a new class identity of upper class and new money families.[191]

Since Colorado was not a state prior to the commencement of the Gilded Age, a formalized high society was not something that was inherently established. Louise Sneed Hill's mission to cement the city of Denver as a valued social capital of the United States was derived and inspired by those great societies in the East. Mrs. Astor's 400, a society for the privileged class, was the example of aristocratic success in America, and it was a model by which Hill was able to pattern her society while modifying it to suit her vision of gentility and her western surroundings.

4

REFORMING THE SOCIAL WASTELAND

Those with new money—the arrivistes, or nouveau riche, as they were often referred to—were those families who had very recently acquired wealth or those who appeared to be "typically perceived as ostentatious or lacking in good taste."[192] Many in high society defined the nouveau riche in this manner due to the belief that "respectable women [and men] were not supposed to lead lives of unashamed luxury."[193] In other words, the nouveau riche were flashy, unpolished, very rich and, yet, still strived for the same recognition as those of old money within their city's high society social scene. As author Larry May discussed in his book *Screening Out the Past*, "nothing characterized the urban press of the 1890s more than a disdain for the lavish, seemingly decadent behavior unfolding on New York's Fifth Avenue."[194] This conduct was embodied by the nouveau riche across the country.

May King Van Rensselaer, a Knickerbocker woman, once wrote about the appearance of the nouveau riche in New York City and said that "all at once, society was assailed from every side by persons who sought to climb boldly over the walls of social exclusiveness."[195] She continued, in her book *The Social Ladder*, to differentiate further by saying that those of old money "knew the history of the families with which they had associated for generations, and these histories were vital parts of the record of the city in which they lived. The segments of the social circle were held together by intimate ties, and this intimacy made of the social organization a clan into which few might expect to force their way."[196] Van Rensselaer's sentiments were shared by many of those who also considered themselves old money, including Louise Hill, who reportedly routinely denied Denver socialite and philanthropist Margaret Brown entrance into the Sacred 36. Historians have speculated that Hill denied Brown because of Brown's unrefined behavior, new money status and poor Irish Catholic origins. The Irish sentiment cannot be accurate, as Hill welcomed formerly poor Irishman Thomas Walsh and his family to her social events and her social register (his daughter, Evalyn, was at the top of Hill's list for eligible young ladies in society). She even stated in her article for *Harper's Bazaar* that the Walsh family had the most beautiful country house of all Colorado's fashionable elite.[197] It seems reasonable to assume that Hill may have not appreciated Brown's perceived abrasiveness, or unwillingness to assimilate to high society etiquette, as Hill defined it, or that Hill simply did not enjoy Brown's company. Although they had their differences, Brown and Hill both supported philanthropic foundations, such as the Babies' Summer Hospital.[198] After Brown survived the sinking of the *Titanic*, Hill extended an olive branch and honored the "heroine of the *Titanic*," who had never been invited to "cross the threshold of the 'great white square' or to break bread with its mistress" at a luncheon with a coterie of Hill's friends at the Denver Country Club on May 1, 1912. According to the *Denver Post*, with that event, the 36 "vindicated itself and proved that the open sesame to its sacred circles is neither money nor social prestige; that a splendid action calls forth a quick response from the impulsive leader."[199]

While there was no formal membership process for entering the Sacred 36, many assumed at the time that money was the key factor in deciding

The Crawford Hills at a gathering with the Walsh family at Wolhurst in Littleton, Colorado, in 1907. Evalyn Walsh (pictured here in the year before her marriage to Edward McLean) was famous for being the last private owner of the Hope Diamond. Here, she is standing in the front, wearing a bright colored dress and holding a puppy. *Courtesy of the Denver Public Library, Western History Collection, X-12117.*

who was worthy of the sacred title. In 1913, when asked directly about the requirements for gaining the seal of approval to join the group (specifically, if the main requirement was wealth), Hill stated (reportedly in horror), "Money! Certainly not! Just look over the so-called list of the 36 and see how very small a part money plays. Very few of the 36 (I quote the popular description of my friends and myself) are rich. And then think of the enormously wealthy people who are not in society."[200] She plainly stated in another article that money had nothing to do with one's social position in Denver; she wrote that, "except for a dozen or more prominent and wealthy families, smart society [was] not composed of the richest people."[201]

While Astor's 400 list was derived solely from prestigious family names and immense wealth, over time, Hill's 36 was different. The 36 was not made up of individuals who possessed titles or impressive ancestral ties. Over the decades of its existence, some of the members of the 36 included:

- *Mr. and Mrs. Charles McAllister Willcox (a Denver capitalist, treasurer of the Denver Press Club, vice-president and general manager of the Daniels and Fisher department store)*
- *Mr. and Mrs. P. Randolph Morris (railroad businessman)*
- *Mr. and Mrs. George B. Berger (president of the Colorado National Bank and first husband of Crawford Hill's sister, Gertrude)*
- *Mr. and Mrs. E.C. Stimson (a Denver judge)*
- *Mr. and Mrs. Lucius Cuthbert (an attorney for the Colorado Midland Railway Company; the Atchison, Topeka, and Kansas Railway Company; and others, also the second husband of Crawford Hill's sister, Gertrude)*
- *Mr. and Mrs. W.C. Russell (Denver mining engineer)*
- *Mr. and Mrs. T.B. Stearns (founder of the Stearns-Roger Manufacturing Company)*
- *Mr. and Mrs. William Cooke Daniels (son of William B. Daniels, who founded Daniels and Fisher Department Store—William Cooke took over ownership of the store in 1891)*
- *Mr. and Mrs. Edward Marsden Cook (stock manager at Daniels and Fisher)*
- *Mr. and Mrs. Theodore Holland (real estate)*
- *Orlando Willcox (brother of Charles Wilcox, Civil War general and colonel and lawyer)*
- *Mr. and Mrs. Chester Beatty (mining engineer with connections to New York and London)*

- *Mr. and Mrs. T.A Richards (clerk for Hornblower and Weeks)*
- *Mr. and Mrs. Benjamin "B.B." Lawrence (mining engineer, president of the Smuggler-Union Mining Company)*
- *Mr. and Mrs. Daniel Tears (lawyer for the New York Central Railroad)*
- *Bulkeley Wells (polo player, mining investor and president of the Smuggler-Union Gold Mine)*

The 36 were also responsible for the establishment of the Denver Country Club in 1901, the Mile High Club in 1902 and the Cactus Club in 1911, which were "all exclusive and highly contributory aggregations to social and cultural Denver."[202] While Hill stated that money did not deem entrance into the 36, based on the careers of some of the known members, that does not necessarily seem to be the case. While all members of the 36 may not have been nearly as wealthy as the Hills, that did not mean they were of the economic middle class or working class. It appears that most of the named members were prominent in their own genres of business,

A dinner party for the Sacred 36 at the Denver Country Club. *Courtesy of the Denver Public Library, Western History Collection, X-29430.*

which provided them with connections and wealth—both of which aided them in earning the sacred distinction.

Hill once again echoed Van Rensselaer's earlier sentiments in a 1926 article, when she discussed the difference between American and European society. Hill found European aristocracy preferable to the American equivalent. Hill stated that one of the biggest differences between the two was the "potency of American riches" and the ostentatious nature of the new-money Americans. She believed it was perhaps "the newness of our country and the sudden obligations that quick wealth impose that make for a type of self-important Yankee, much too numerous these days in our commonwealth."[203]

Due to this distinction within genteel class identity, there was a large movement for young, wealthy, American women to marry gentlemen of British peerage. In essence, these young ladies were entering a business agreement. They traded their wealth for a desirable title and undeniable, irrefutable entrance into any high society they wished. Transatlantic marriage migration was a particularly popular choice for the nouveau riche. Unable to gain entrance into high society due to their familial backgrounds and lack of high societal upbringing, ladies of the nouveau riche were rather forced to travel abroad in order to find suitable marriage prospects. While this was far more prevalent in New York than in Colorado, the idea of a hierarchy within the upper echelon of society was something that Louise Hill firmly cemented from the very beginning of Denver high society. She believed that European society was something that should be emulated in America, as there were "fewer snobs" in the European aristocracy than in American society. Hill felt that Europeans possessed a "virtue of an ancient and established [tradition]," they were "reared for generations in opulence," but those "exalted Europeans" were still "simple souls, totally unimpressed with their importance."[204] In a time of pretentious, flamboyant nouveau riche, to be simply elegant, gracious and to emulate traditional aristocracy was highly important to the old money individuals. It was how they were distinguished from their less genteel counterparts.

Margaret Brown was not the only woman "denied" entrance into the 36 due to her inability to fit the certain criteria required; there were at least two hundred other couples who were considered to be of an upper social class but who were not worthy of the elite distinction. Hill felt that there were "so many nouveau riche living in the most expensive and richly furnished houses," but just as in New York, they had "no place in Denver's social world."[205] These social constructs were expressly declared in a work

Louise Hill designed herself. Though she often referred to sociability as a game, rather implying that anyone could "win" in opposition of the strict rules of a hierarchy, she still maintained a sense of order by restricting behaviors and developing a set of rules and strategies that individuals could follow in order to enter the arena of elite sociability. Though it appeared to be an open call, a more democratic and individualistic way to approach elite society that allowed others to create their social identities, not everyone could play the game. Only individuals who were prepared with the proper tools could make their way into the tournament that was the contest of elite sociability.

Louise Hill provided avenues and suggestions on how individuals could attain these attributes in her published work. Much like the social register that was published in New York City, which defined the list of the 400 and "establish[ed] the border separating the aristocrat from the parvenu," Hill's book *Who's Who in Denver Society* sought to serve the same purpose.[206] The book, which was originally bound in red cloth with gold lettering, was published in 1908. In its pages, Mrs. Crawford Hill told "the rest of the salt of the Earth just where they belong[ed]."[207] The book, which was arranged like a "birthday cake, in various layers," contained society in a "new alignment," personally "censored" by Mrs. Hill.[208] It contained the many names of those individuals in Denver who were considered to be of an upper class. Naturally, Hill put herself and her husband, Crawford, at the top of the list for the category titled "The Smart Set," along with members of her family and the Sacred 36. Those named at the top of the list included Mr. and Mrs. Thomas F. Walsh (a mining-magnate-turned-philanthropist and an influential businessman in Washington, D.C.) and Mr. and Mrs. L.M. Cuthbert (Crawford Hill's sister).[209] At the conclusion of the work was a category titled "Others," where the names of many individuals who "really thought they were in society" were classified.[210]

According to the text, some "hints on behavior" suggested that "manners are indeed stronger than laws and are signs by which one's status is fixed." The text continued, stating that people of breeding never "look up to" or "look down upon" their associates but, rather, they leave them with the effect of "unspoken caress without the familiarity of anything personal." The book also states that to "be quietly *qui vive* is the first mark of breeding." These traits, along with countless others, including the avoidance of painful or disgusting topics and laughing or giggling, were the set requirements that all individuals—both men and women—who hoped to enter the upper echelons of society must possess.[211]

Many of the rules set forth in Louise Hill's book required the women of high society to be intelligent and quick-witted, constantly on the lookout for various situations to arise while maintaining their composure and high level of manners consistent with proper breeding and respectable pedigree. Before and during the Gilded Age, women were the epitome of the top principles of the class order. One way these women asserted their individual identities and ushered in the modern era was their public displays of cultural capital, both in person and in newspaper articles. The cultural capital they possessed was uniquely theirs, and it did not belong to their husbands or any other males of their class. They utilized this asset to create their class, perpetuate a sense of superiority and as "a rite of sociability."[212] Many newspaper articles published about the high society women of this time discussed their choices of clothing, the trips they took and the events they attended and hosted. Much of the time, women achieved their prominent positions through spending and exhibiting their cultural capital to the public. These class-motivated societal factors all contributed to Louise Hill's mindset in her formation of the Sacred 36.

By creating personal connections with newspaper reporters, influencing them to feature her parties and attire in their writing, spending excessive amounts of money on her clothing and soirees, traveling internationally to attend society events and purchasing an apartment on Park Avenue in New York, it was clear that Hill wanted her modern society to be internationally recognized and legitimized. These actions resulted in personal achievements for Hill, which perhaps included entrance into New York's high society (the 400), and in Gilded Age America, an invitation to Mrs. Astor's ballroom meant true success and acceptance for a woman of Hill's class and stature.

COLORADO NEWSPAPERS, A LOVE AFFAIR

By positioning herself as a gatekeeper for Denver's social elite, Louise Hill followed the example of New York's leading female socialite, Caroline Schermerhorn Astor. New York City quickly turned into the place to be for members of high society during the Gilded Age. As historian Eric Homberger stated, the "tone of social life in New York was shaped by a distinctive passion for aristocracy."[213] Astor threw lavish balls, inviting only individuals of high sophistication and old money, and those who accepted her invitations sought to "occupy a position of enhanced sociability."[214] If an individual's name was not on the list, they did not have a prayer for having any sort of debut in high society. As it was previously stated, Astor had very strict guidelines for her social events and viewed new money families as—in the words of author Greg King—"uncouth parvenus."[215] Astor orchestrated many events, including grand balls that were held in her own personal ballroom at her home. These balls, which were modeled after those common in British aristocracy, were intended to be occasions where one could socialize, and parents could introduce their daughters into high society.[216] It was important for those of great wealth to marry individuals of the same caliber, class and comparable lineage in order to maintain the sense of exclusivity the upper echelons of society were known for. Astor's exclusive 400 list, so named as four hundred was the capacity of her ballroom, provided the best way for rich New Yorkers to perpetuate the cycle of exclusivity that had been established. Astor's social gatherings were frequently chronicled in the society pages of New York's newspapers, including the *New York Times*. The society pages of the *New York Times* provided her a platform on which to display the exclusivity of her events.[217]

There grew a "hunger for information about aristocratic circles" due to the intense fascination of the public consumers with the clothing, actions, betrothals, dissolutions and palatial residences of the American aristocracy.[218] The society pages granted the general public a place to satiate their thirst for information, but it also brought about a new requirement for the women of high society with social aspirations: publicity management. Louise Hill took the cue from Astor's society page features and began a love affair with the society pages of Colorado's various newspapers on her wedding day that lasted through her dying day. The idea of publicity management, however, lends itself to the line of demarcation between the social careers of Astor and Hill. Hill managed her own public image; she very frequently gave interviews and fostered close, personal relationships with journalists. Astor, on the other hand, never once gave an interview during her societal reign. Hill was also the sole creator and arbiter of her social scene, while Astor had assistance with the 400. A man named Ward McAllister was the one who coined the term "400" (for marketing purposes), and it was McAllister who cultivated relationships with the press of New York City and spoke publicly for Astor and the folks of Fifth Avenue. That is not to say that Astor was not involved in maintaining and creating the 400 society, as Homberger stated, it is difficult "in any social sense to see what particular need Mrs. Astor had for McAllister," as she was capable of handling all matters herself.[219] Nevertheless, McAllister was involved in the publicity management and marketing of the 400 and the New York aristocracy, while Louise Hill accomplished her societal career completely on her own, without the aid of a public relations manager—clearly, another instance in which Hill had a more modern mind-set.

Perhaps part of Hill's ability to manage her image in the press stemmed from her husband's family's ownership of a local newspaper. Louise's husband, Crawford Hill, inherited ownership of the Republican Publishing Company, which published the newspaper the *Denver Republican*, from his father. It is highly plausible that the knowledge Louise gained from the publication gave her insight on how to best market herself in order to stay at the forefront of breaking society news. It was important for her to stay in the limelight—to represent herself to the outside world in such a manner that she characterized the ideal woman. Though she claimed in early interviews that she did not want to appear to be on a higher plane than the rest of Denver's citizens, in pursuance of perpetuating exclusivity, she had to maintain a sense of unattainable wealth, prominence and societal etiquette. In order to do this in a society she deemed undeveloped, Hill implemented her ideas of a modern genteel woman and what she believed to be proper behavior (culturally speaking) on the citizens of Denver. By modeling her ideals after Mrs. Astor's 400 and her own idea of gentility, rather than the previous ideals of early Denver (which relied on Victorian culture alone), she changed the structure of elite sociability and was able to sustain a legacy for herself that was unmatched by any other Denver citizen of her time.

Hill began her rise to the top by seeking to, as Kristen Iversen quoted in her work *Molly Brown*, "captivate all of Denver with her charm, wit, and beauty."[220] Unlike the old guard of Denver, Hill had an affinity for the press and invited the various news outlets to write about her. She welcomed attention—craved it, even—and wanted to be seen by everyone, everywhere. The press was an important piece of Denver society, according to Hill. She set out to foster a social environment in which newspaper reporters could "walk in and out of houses in an intimate way." She hoped that it would create more "democratic" society columns in the local papers. Further distinguishing Hill's society from those in the East, Hill asserted that, "unlike New York and London papers," those of Denver were of a modern mind-set, and they "accepted the facts and people as they [were] and not as they would [have] liked to have them."[221]

Historians have previously asserted that Crawford and Louise lived in La Veta Place (a row of Victorian brownstone apartments on the southwest corner of West Colfax Avenue and Bannock Street) after their marriage.

That is actually not the case, though the mix-up is understandable. La Veta Place was the most elegant apartment house in Denver. Built in the 1880s by financier and industrialist David Moffat, the structure was later purchased by "Silver King" Horace Tabor (Augusta Tabor, his ex-wife, then received ownership of the property in their divorce settlement). Prominent Denver citizens, such as Dennis Sullivan, a founder of Denver National Bank, and others of that caliber, resided within the walls of the castle-like La Veta Place. It was a social landmark for Denver's high society. There were countless social functions, including balls, receptions and parties, held for the fashionable elite at La Veta Place. The brownstones began to fall into disrepair by 1901.

In 1902, the Denver Public Library acquired the property and surrounding land for $98,000, and it housed its collections there. The library intended to refurbish the handsome structure but received a new grant to build a Carnegie library that same year. La Veta Place was razed in 1909 to make room for Civic Center Park. With the prominence that La Veta Place held in the community as a residence, it is reasonable to see why individuals thought the Hills lived there. The apartment house was also across the street from where the Hills actually made their home, 1407 Cleveland Place. The house

La Veta Place, circa 1890, was the most handsome apartment complex in the city of Denver at the time. Built in the 1880s, it was later owned by Colorado's "Silver King" Horace Tabor. *Courtesy of the Denver Public Library, Western History Collection, WHJ-10348.*

at 1407 Cleveland Place was the former home of Thomas H. Lawrence and his family, who lived in the residence from about 1888 until the start of 1895. Lawrence was known as "one of the most intelligent and successful cattlemen of the plains" and at one time or another owned or managed various ranches and cattle companies.[222] He operated an office in Denver out of the Barclay Block on Larimer Street. His wife, Kate, was active in the early Denver social scene and entertained members of Denver's old guard at their home, including Mrs. Bethel.[223]

In March 1895, Nathaniel P. Hill purchased the Lawrence's home for his son and daughter-in-law. In April 1900, Crawford Hill took possession of the property, a month before his father's death. The Crawford Hills hired the architecture firm of Boal and Harnois to repair and alter their Cleveland Place home over the years they lived there, but after the birth of their sons, Nathaniel in 1896 and Crawford Jr. in 1898, the Hills decided the home no longer suited their needs.[224] After the Hills moved out of their Cleveland Place home, they rented the property to the Denver Republican Club, the Denver Motor Club, the Democratic Club and the Foo and Wing Herb Co.[225]

The Hills built a French Renaissance mansion on the corner of Tenth and Sherman Streets. Crawford Hill gained possession of the property on November 29, 1904. The construction of the three-story, single-family dwelling was started in 1905 and completed in 1906. The immense residence cost $35,000 (roughly $1 million in today's dollars) and was designed by the architecture firm of Boal and Harnois. Theodore Davis Boal, a prominent architect in Denver, is one reason the home is so important today. Boal designed some of the most important structures in early Denver; some of his most well-known projects include: Grant Humphreys Mansion, St. Peter's Episcopal Church, Lowell Elementary School and Osgood Castle.

The seventeen-thousand-square-foot mansion has impressive architectural features, including classically symmetrical proportions, columns, rounded dormers and arched windows. The interior of the home contains twenty-two (noted in some publications as twenty-three) rooms and nine fireplaces. The first floor comprised the dining room and other gathering spaces, the second floor contained multiple bedrooms and the third floor was utilized as servant's quarters. Although the front door faced Tenth Avenue, the Hills preferred to use the address 969 Sherman Street. Sherman Street led directly to the state capitol building and having a home on that street implied a sense of political and social stature within the community.[226]

Left: Five-year-old Nathaniel P. Hill IV. *Courtesy of History Colorado, accession #90.314.376.*

Right: Crawford Hill Jr. in 1903. *Courtesy of History Colorado, accession #90.314.84.*

Exterior of the Louise and Crawford Hill Mansion. *Courtesy of the Denver Public Library, Western History Collection, X-26653.*

Interior of the Crawford Hill Mansion. Both the chandelier and mirror still exist in the structure. *Courtesy of the Denver Public Library, Western History Collection, Z-6895.*

The "Corner Hall" of the Hill Mansion, which is located on the corner of Tenth and Sherman Streets. *Courtesy of History Colorado, accession #90.314.82.*

Louise Hill designed the interior of her home and chose the furnishings herself. In 1905, she traveled overseas to acquire rich draperies, costly ornamentation, rare old mahogany, soft toned Bokhara rugs, rare tapestries, bits of ivory and paintings to decorate the interior of her home. The *Rocky Mountain News* declared in 1905 that the Hills' mansion was the most elegantly furnished and most artistic home in Denver. Local newspapers could not get enough of the home that would have been considered "a good house in Paris or London," and columnists declared it was the perfect replica of an old French palace.[227]

CREATING THE LEGACY

Hill attended all sorts of social functions in Denver in the hopes of establishing herself as the city's reigning queen, and she began holding social events at her new mansion as well. One of her first acts as the self-titled social arbiter of Denver was to declare forty names that she considered to be worthy of high society. An untitled newspaper article in a scrapbook that resides within the Louise Hill collection stated the "immaculate, immortal forty [were] tagged and ribboned beyond the peradventure of a doubt." These names were those individuals who were exclusively in attendance at a dance at the Adams Hotel. Mrs. Crawford Hill, the article relayed, was "IT." The article named all forty guests, and concluded by stating, "And there you are—or are not!"[228]

Perhaps knowingly or not, Hill whittled down the forty names to thirty-six herself. She began hosting bridge parties in her stately home and instructed others in "the best way to arrange the tables," but she said to "be sure and do not say that [she] arranged the tables."[229] Like Mrs. Astor's New York ballroom, which could only fit four hundred people, Mrs. Hill's society was named after the capacity of her bridge tables. Hill's bridge parties were exclusive and consisted of nine tables of four players each—hence, the 36 was born.

Historians have often attributed the "sacred" title of the 36 to an untitled newspaper interview that a journalist conducted with Louisa Hughes Morris. Morris was one of Louise's closest friends (whom Louise considered herself to be inseparable from) and "whom she [had] known for many years."[230] Supposedly, Morris responded to a journalist's question by stating: "Goodness, you'd think we were sacred, the way you were asking." The

Mrs. Crawford Hill (in the front left of the photograph with a large flower arrangement on her shoulder) threw a party for the Sacred Thirty-Six at the Denver Country Club around 1914 or 1915. Caroline Bancroft (a Denver historian whose parents were members of the sacred circle) knew Mrs. Hill and the other members personally, and she wrote in the names of the individuals present. *Courtesy of the Denver Public Library, Western History Collection, X-19820.*

journalist properly titled the story that followed "Party at Mrs. Hill's for the Sacred 36" and the general public referred to the group of social elites as such from that moment forward.[231]

Hill found success as the doyenne of Denver society. It was important for her to stay in the limelight and to represent herself to the outside world as the ideal, modern woman. She always kept things interesting with new ideas and ways to market herself in the press. One society article reported that Hill attended various theater performances, and at times, when shows began, she would stand and face the audience rather than the stage so that the audience could gaze on her as well. [232]

Throughout her time as the self-designated reigning queen of Denver society, Hill penned letters to various newspaper reporters at numerous establishments, including the *Rocky Mountain News*. She instructed them on how to portray her in the society pages and, at times, bribed them to do so. According to a 1955 *Post* article, Hill once gave a brooch comprised of emeralds and diamonds to a society columnist who composed a "particularly glowing" article about her.[233] In a letter to Miss Helen Eastom of the *Denver Post*, Hill expressed her deepest regrets of not being able to come into her office, for she was far too busy but still wanted to present her with a photograph, "which [was] really lovely except the face, which does not look like a human being." Hill went on to instruct Eastom to "tell the printer who executes the picture that you put in the paper, that if he will have the face blurred…he will do me an everlasting favor and I shall properly send him a check for $5.00." Hill also said, "Mr. Bonfils will think it is only a mistake, and the picture will be divine." Included in the letter, Hill sent the lines of wording to accompany the photograph. Hill's lines described her as "too magnificent" and instructed Eastom that if she didn't use them, Hill understood; however, if she recalled correctly, Eastom told her to write the lines in such a way as to make herself sound like "the greatest person in the world."[234] It was encounters like this one that aided Hill's rise to the top.[235] In fact, every week, the Sunday issue of the *Denver Republican* featured the comings and goings of Mrs. Crawford Hill in the top articles of the society pages.

Though Hill was able to control many publications through bribes and ownerships, it seems she did not have the support of one of the *Denver Post's* most popular writers, "Polly Pry."[236] In a pointed letter from an individual at the Polly Pry Publishing Company (most likely "Polly Pry" herself) to what appears to be a person employed at the *Republican*, the individual from the publishing company relayed her frustration with the constant feature of Mrs. Hill in the society pages. Pry stated in her letter that she had enclosed a copy of the previous week's *Sunday Republican* and, to her dismay, the first five stories on the society pages were about Louise Hill, and her name appeared six times in the seven stories present for that section. Pry wrote: "[I] read the society pages every Sunday and want to ask if it is fair to the rest of the people of Denver that we should be punished this way every Sunday?" Pry also mentioned that one long-standing society editor (whose name is never revealed in the letter) had recently been fired from the *Republican* for not putting Hill's name first in the first item for one edition of the paper. In conclusion, Pry requested that the recipient of her letter take her concerns up to their superiors to "get us some relief." She thought it was "ridiculous" to feature the Hills so regularly in the paper; she also felt that the Hills were not nearly interesting enough to warrant all of the stories about them.

She stated, "If Mr. or Mrs. Hill had any distinction aside from owning the *Republican* and having money," the constant bombardment of stories about them "might be not quite so tiresome." Further cementing her position, Pry stated that she had felt that way for a while and would have written to this person about it sooner, but she "thought their pride would have stopped it without having to appeal to someone else."[237]

In return, the recipient of the letter retaliated with a letter of his or her own, stating "sorry to disagree with you, the *Republican* is owned by the Hills…recognized social leaders of Denver." He or she argued that it was preposterous to think that Mrs. Hill would not be featured in the first articles of the society page, as it was "the place in which the doings of the fashionably elect of Denver are chronicled," and as the social leader of Denver, Hill would, of course, be included in that. He or she continued, writing that, in New York City, "an annual Astor ball is required for the establishment of social lines.…In Denver, the same result is accomplished fifty-two times a year by the *Sunday Republican.*"[238] The assertion in that particular passage is clear. Just as Mrs. Astor had gatherings that cemented her status as reigning queen in New York, Louise Hill did the same in Denver with the aid of the weekly publications that praised her actions, style and soirées.

This letter is an example of a clear difference between the relationships that existed in New York and Denver between the society leaders and the individuals of the press. There's a certain sense of a more intimate bond and a necessity to establish Hill's prominence through prolific features in Denver's society pages. Continuing, the author of the letter further defended the Hills by writing a short personal history of the Hill family. The writing, while praising Louise Hill's pedigree, warned those who were unprepared to deal with the iron fist of her reign. The author wrote:

> As long as there must be class distinctions, there will be a sacred inner circle, and Denver is to be congratulated on the fact that its leading society family is rich, refined and well-bred. My advice…cease reading the society page of the Republican.…Society is a queer game, and if you are not in it, you should be prepared to play it for all there is in it.

The author went on to write that "philosophy considered, it is a disease… it exists, has its votaries, high priests, neophytes and victims, and if you butt up against it…beware of the carom."[239] This rather public quarrel between Pry and Hill could very well have been a publicity stunt. According to Chuck Bonniwell and David Fridtjof Halaas in their work *The History of the Denver*

Country Club, Leonel Ross Campbell Anthony (who went by the pen name Polly Pry in her profession) actually "enjoyed lunching" with Hill at the Denver Country Club—and Margaret Brown, whom she also squabbled with publicly.[240] They also wrote that Pry and Hill were "fast friends" and that Hill could "count on press coverage in the *Post* (the paper where Pry wrote the society column) that was not afforded anyone else in society."[241]

Hill continued to grace the society pages of various Denver publications, whether it was in articles about her tiara that "dazzled society" and oozed with diamonds, her diet regimen of "two glasses of buttermilk, two crackers, and water" or giving up "letting her friends copy everything she wears or does" for Lent.[242] During Hill's time, women were "the exclusive bearers of aesthetic taste and refinement…destined to be the agent[s] of culture and moral perfection."[243] Hill used the display of her cultural capital to maintain the air of importance and set the tone for her upper crust society. At times, Hill hoped to appear relatable to a larger audience as well. Local newspapers published articles that described her "human qualities," which truly made her status seem that much more unreachable. She was depicted as being the symbol of elite perfection while also being humble and relatable. In her own words, Hill felt it was her "aptitude for doing the charming and graceful thing, [her] ready sympathy for others, a naturalness of manner as refreshing as a spring, tact breeding and an uncanny sense of the fitness of things, and a proficient memory remembering the little personal feelings between people and avoiding situations that might result in friction" that were all factors of her success as a contemporary woman of high society.[244]

One of Hill's supposed eccentricities—most likely a simple publicity stunt (but one that stuck nonetheless)—was the assertion that she only ever wore the colors black or white. *Denver Post* columnists reported in 1912 that Mrs. Hill "seldom [wore] anything but black and white or a combination of the two." This was not the case; though it created quite a buzz about Hill for years to come. Every time she wore a color other than black or white, it created a bit of a frenzy in the society pages. Hill created this image for herself as a clear attempt to gain publicity, focus attention on herself and set herself apart from the rest of society—it worked. Another undated article in the Louise Hill collection scrapbook, a clipping titled "The Box Occupants," discussed the preconceived notion that Mrs. Hill "never [appeared] in anything but black or white or black and white." The author stated they felt that eccentricity was a sign of her brilliance, as "nothing else could so well enhance the beauty of her luminous clear white complexion and dark eyes and hair." The

Mrs. Crawford Hill, seen here in an extravagant headpiece on March 16, 1914, was not afraid to push the boundaries of what was appropriate, socially speaking, including when it came to her manner of dress. *Courtesy of the Denver Public Library, Western History Collection, F22466.*

author went on to write that, as they sat admiring her from afar, they tried to picture what Hill would look like in different colors, such as pink, purple, blue or red but, then, "shuddered at the thought of the extent to which they would detract from her perpetual charm."[245] Hill, in fact, wore many different colors quite frequently, including maroon, Irish green and gold.

Hill used the press to further the modernization of Denver society as well. Local newspaper outlets featured stories of Mrs. Hill's innovative ideas and parties. Hill once again emulated her eastern counterparts by implementing costume balls in Denver. The tradition of costume balls in New York was revamped in the 1840s by the Knickerbocker families.[246] In the 1890s, the tradition of costume balls was still in full swing, as represented by the incredibly lavish Bradley Martin Ball of 1897. About 1,200 guests were invited to the "age of Louis XV" themed extravaganza that became known as one of the most expensive parties ever thrown. The bill for the festive occasion was estimated to be around $270,000 (roughly $8 million in today's currency).[247]

Denver's modern spin on the costume ball, and Louise Hill's influence on society, was apparent during the 1912 Arian Ball that took place on April 12 of that year. The children's hospital was the beneficiary of all the proceeds, and the event was put together by many influential individuals in the city of Denver, including members of the Sacred 36.[248] Unlike the balls of the East, which hearkened back to the past for costume ideas and themes, Denver's Arian Ball evoked a modern time. High society folks who attended the function dressed as champagne bottles, cigarette girls and a "Queen of the Moulin Rouge." Hill dressed as a mermaid for the event and wore silver fish scales, "no bodice" and pearl earrings. Furthering the modern mindset, the article also noted that her husband, Crawford, would be accompanying his wife, not that Hill would be attending with her husband.[249]

Hill was also responsible for many firsts in Denver society, like breakfast balls, parties that did not end until 6:00 a.m., private banquets where an orchestra played during the meal and an afternoon dance where guests frolicked to the "turkey trot" and the "worm wiggle."[250] Historian Marilyn Griggs Riley mentioned in her research that the *Republican* once noted, while most men in the 36 belonged to the "busy rich," they did everything they could to attend Mrs. Hill's morning shindigs. The working men supposedly racked "their brains as to how they [were] going to get down to the office and not miss the dance in the morning. They demand[ed] invitations be for 7:00 a.m.," which would "give them at least an hour for dancing."[251]

Like the flappers of a later decade, Hill pushed the boundaries of what was socially acceptable when it came to alcohol consumption and dance styles. Truly, the flappers were merely following in the footsteps of the generation before them, of which Louise Hill was a headline-making member. One of the dance styles Hill debuted in the Denver social scene was deemed so controversial and wild that it was banned by the White House. In 1910, one of the most popular "animal dances," the turkey trot, was considered so outrageous that doctors warned of the harm it could bring. It was not only banned in multiple cities, but it was "denounced by President Woodrow Wilson."[252] It was considered to be "absolutely vulgar," and those individuals who dared to dance its suggestive steps (or participated in, as New York's former mayor William Jay Gaynor referred to it, the "lascivious orgy") were at risk of being arrested.[253]

Hill was also a forward thinker, politically speaking. She felt that Denver women were not only "charming, cheerful, much traveled" and well-read but were also "interested in all the questions of the day, and more especially in politics." In 1893, Colorado was the first state to enact women's suffrage by popular referendum, and Hill was not only proud of that fact but remained an active supporter of women's rights throughout the 1910s, until the passage of the Nineteenth Amendment. In 1910, Hill stated that she felt women's interest in politics was vital in Colorado, because they had the vote and the right to hold office. Females in the legislature, males elected by female votes and women as candidates for congress were all the "result of the Colorado woman's political career." Hill felt there was a "spirit of comradeship" between the sexes in Colorado and that Colorado men, even though they saw women asserting their independence particularly in the practice of voting, "still [stayed] and worshiped at her shrine."[254]

While Louise Hill was contradictory in some or even most of her behaviors (also in her speech, as she once said, early in her societal reign, that she did not consider society as a profession but later stated it was one of the most difficult jobs), her participation in frivolous acts, such as roller-skating and the introduction of a nationally inappropriate dance like the turkey trot, cemented her place as a forward-thinking woman intent on revolutionizing local and national society and ushering America into a more modern era.

5

BOLD AND BRAZEN MRS. HILL

Under the reign of Victorianism, sexuality was repressed; women were "implored to control themselves, particularly their sensual natures."[255] If a woman was to remain in high standing within her community and social class, she had to remain pure and resist the allure of drinking, games and sexual pleasures. Victorian women had to "guard against high spirits, for fallen women lost caste and could be contaminated with disease."[256] Respectable Victorian women were consistently chaperoned when attending any event outside of their homes that did not involve church or paying a social call on another society woman. Women who visited areas where drinking, fervent dancing or other risqué activities took place risked "threatening their familial as well as economic status."[257] As Henry Seidel Canby stated in his work *The Age of Confidence: Life in the Nineties*:

> *A girl at a ball was a woman on show, a custodian of honor and the home who could flirt and be gay and tease and be teased, but one hint of the sexual made her "common," which was only one word above "vulgar."*

As has been previously stated, the Gilded Age saw a shift in gender roles as more women entered the public sphere. In her attempts to usher in the modern age, Louise Hill did not shy away from revising the social norms. She not only frequently went out unescorted, but she also went so far as to have a publicly known—though never reported in the press—love affair. She did not repress her sensuality, but she actually gave in to her sexual instincts.

Bulkeley Wells, pictured here, had a long-term love affair with Mrs. Hill while he maintained a close friendship with her husband, Crawford. *Courtesy of History Colorado, accession #90.314.12.*

While it was not publicized in the papers, Louise Hill's affair with Bulkeley Wells was public knowledge to those in her social circle. In Victorian homes, it was common for sexual activities to be kept at a bare minimum. Perhaps Crawford Hill did not fulfill his wife's desires, or maybe, she simply yearned for more. Since "divorce was almost unknown, for unhappiness was no excuse to break up a home," Louise Hill did not separate from her husband but, instead, had an affair with a man whom they both considered to be a close friend and traveling companion.[258]

Throughout their years of marriage, the Hills partially maintained their wealth in the industry Crawford's father had revolutionized: smelting. Due to mutual interests in the success of the mining industry, the Hills found themselves acquainted with Mr. and Mrs. Bulkeley Wells. Bulkeley Wells (1872–1931) was a graduate of the engineering school at Harvard University (class of 1894), and by 1896, he was known on a national scale in the discipline of hydroelectric engineering.[259] He married Grace Livermore, the daughter of successful lawyer and mining investor Colonel Thomas Livermore, and they had four children together over their twenty-three years of marriage. Wells's father-in-law was a major investor in Telluride's "richest and most famous gold mine," and the Wells family settled in Colorado. Wells served as the president and general manager of the Smuggler-Union in Telluride and headed, at minimum, sixty other mining companies as president or director in the states of California, Nevada and Colorado.[260] He served as the president of the American Mining Congress and was also a member of the American Institute of Mining and Metallurgical Engineers. He was once an adjutant-general of Colorado and played an instrumental role in capturing the men who killed former Idaho governor Stunenberg. Due to his role in the investigation, Wells was a target for murder, and in 1908, a bomb was placed under his bed in Telluride, though he escaped serious injury.[261] Wells was also a polo player, and his dashing good looks and suave style certainly attracted the attention of Louise Hill.

The event at which the Hills first made the acquaintance of Bulkeley Wells is unknown; perhaps they met at one of the various social polo events in Denver. Whatever the case, Wells quickly became a close friend of the Hills. Crawford Hill mentioned Wells in quite a few of his personal letters to his sons, Nathaniel and Crawford, while they were away, studying at Harvard.[262] Crawford also penned personal letters to Wells and signed them "as ever devotedly your friend."[263] All the while, Louise Hill and Bulkeley engaged in a love affair. As mentioned in a previous chapter, at the Arian Ball of 1912, Louise Hill's mermaid costume did not match that of her husband, who dressed in a court costume; rather, it went nicely with the costume of her lover, who dressed as the "lone fisherman," though the article noted he was "just playing the part, you understand, not really."[264] On September 14, 1914, Hill also attended a polo luncheon thrown by Wells at the Denver Country Club, sans her husband.

The Wells family lived in Colorado Springs, but by 1914, Bulkeley Wells had his own office and apartment in the city of Denver. Wells and the Hills were all members of the Denver Country Club. Partygoers at the various dances and events of the club remembered Wells and Mrs. Hill leaving the dance together to "disappear upstairs."[265] Crawford either did not notice or did not mind the affair—some individuals who knew him, such as Caroline Bancroft, said he was dull and not very bright— as they continued to be a tight trio of travel partners and even spent winters in Palm Beach, Florida, together.[266] When their sons had trouble abroad or in school, Mr. Hill frequently enlisted Wells's assistance in the matters.[267] In fact, their bond became so tight that Mrs. Hill hung a life-sized portrait of their dear friend Wells in his finest polo attire beside her husband Crawford's smaller, head-only portrait in the main foyer of their Sherman Street mansion.

On display in the foyer of the Hill's Sherman Street mansion was a smaller, head-only portrait of Crawford Hill. It was accompanied by a much larger, full-body depiction of Bulkeley Wells, Louise Hill's lover, in his finest polo attire. *Courtesy of the Denver Public Library, Western History Collection, Z-6890.*

The Hills and Wells families had a very close relationship that extended to their children, and young Nathaniel and Crawford Hill Jr. thought very highly of Mr. Bulkeley Wells. In a ten-page letter to his mother, dated April 25, 1912, Nathaniel P. Hill IV (who was in Rhode Island studying at St. George's School at the time) detailed his school activities and his desire to please his mother, and he brought up Bulkeley Wells. Nathaniel told his mother of his intention to join a club at school that he felt would help him develop into an "attractive man" (something he very much desired), and to him, an attractive man was one who could "hold your interest when talking to you." In order to do that, a man had to be "well read" and "well informed." He went on to relay that he meant the "most attractive man [was], as a rule, the man who [knew] a little bit about everything" and was "able to talk easily with you on any subject that you are interested in and may bring up." The first example of his idea of an attractive man was Wells. He wrote:

Take, for example, Bulkeley Wells. I shouldn't suggest that he was quite as keen a mathematical thinker as Sir Isaac Newton, but I will wager my hat that he is much more attractive and interesting. I am sure that you will admit that if you are in a mood to talk about books, Bulkeley is very good company, and the same with practically all other subjects, simply because he is so well informed.[268]

It is highly likely that this passage of his letter served two purposes. First, Nathaniel seems to have truly felt that Wells was a well-educated and successful man that he admired; Wells was put in an authoritative position by Louise Hill, which created the image that Wells was someone for her sons to look up to and emulate. Second, Nathaniel Hill sought his mother's approval to join this school club, and by stating that the club would help mold him into a man like his mother's lover, Bulkeley, he was most likely going to win her approval. This was not young Nathaniel's only mention of Wells in his letters home to his mother. Nathaniel also relayed in a March 17, 1912 letter that he was heading to New York and going to the theater, but he said that Louise should not worry, because he had already "told Bulkeley about these arrangements."[269] He wrote to his mother again in 1918 to assure her that he'd been receiving letters from her and Bulkeley while he was serving in the army; all of Nathaniel's letters that year were headed by the description "Office of the Chief of Staff, Headquarters First Army."[270]

The Hill children also vacationed with the Wells children. Bulkeley and Grace Wells had a son, Bulkeley Wells Jr., who was around the same age as Nathaniel Hill. On April 10, 1910, Nathaniel wrote to his younger brother, Crawford (who was still at home in Colorado) while he was away at St. George's School. He penned:

As you know, I spent my vacation with Bulkeley [Jr.] and his grandfather Mr. Livermore. I had a beautiful time....One afternoon, we went out to Arlington to see Bucks' [sic] grandmother Mrs. Wells, who has perallises [sic] and can hardly move....She is one of the dearest old ladies I ever met.[271]

Nathaniel Hill clearly had a very close relationship with not only Bulkeley Jr. (whom he affectionately referred to as "little Bulkeley" in another letter to his mother, dated 1913) but the extended Wells and Livermore families.[272]

In 1918, Wells's wife divorced him and cited desertion as her reason. Wells did not contest the suit and effectively lost his family and the financial backing of his incredibly rich in-laws.[273] In 1919, the Denver City Directory lists Bulkeley Wells as living at 1407 Cleveland Place—the former family home of the Crawford Hills. It is entirely possible that he was living in the Hill's former home that year. Around the same time, Crawford grew very ill. Some described him as an invalid in his final years; he was very sick for a long time, and he either died of heart failure or of a stroke at the age of sixty in 1922.[274]

After Crawford passed, Louise and the rest of Denver society rather expected Wells to marry the widowed Mrs. Hill. Mere weeks after her husband's passing, sixty-year-old Louise Hill was shocked by her lover, as he chose to marry a younger woman instead. A year prior to Crawford's death, Wells had moved to San Francisco in search of new

Crawford Hill, pictured here in his later life, was quite ill during his last few years on Earth. *Courtesy of History Colorado, accession #90.314.71.*

business ventures and met a strawberry-blonde twenty-something-year-old named Virginia Schmidt. They eloped in January 1923, and it appears from the City Directory from that year that Wells and his new bride moved back to Denver and lived on Fourteenth Street. When Hill heard of the union—and, perhaps, after seeing them together in the city she ruled—she severed all ties with her former lover. Supposedly, she convinced some of his financial backers—including the Whitneys of New York, her close friends, whom she had introduced to Wells—to pull their support from Wells. Although Wells's marriage was quite successful (they were together for eight years and had two children together), he was ruined both socially and financially. Wells had once been the manager of the $15 million that Harry Payne Whitney had invested in the West. A newspaper article claimed that after Wells "jilted the woman who had started him out with Whitney," she "got him fired from every job he had" and "made good the old saying that 'hell hath no fury like a woman's scorn.'"[275]

Wells developed a gambling addiction and with a life of poverty in his foreseeable future, he made a drastic decision. He went to his office on the morning of May 26, 1931, spoke briefly with his coworkers and asked for a loan of twenty-five dollars. He returned to his office, sat down at his desk, penned a note to a bookkeeper of his at the Smuggler-Union, took a revolver from his desk, laid down on a couch and shot himself in the head. He lessened the sound of the gunshot by holding a pillow over the pistol, and no one heard the shot. Wells's coworkers entered his office to discuss business and discovered him bleeding out on the couch. Wells was rushed to the hospital, but he never regained consciousness and died shortly thereafter.[276] His suicide note was addressed to his business associate A.D. Snodgrass, and it stated:

> *Dear A.D.—As a result of all my difficulties and worries, I feel that my mind had to go. Either that or a stroke, and I will not be a charge upon anyone. Nothing but bankruptcy is possible as far as my estate is concerned. Do what you can for Mrs. Wells.*
> *—B.W.*[277]

Supposedly, sometime later, Hill held an event for the press at her home. Legend states that her close friend and *Rocky Mountain News* photographer Harry Rhoades pressed Hill to speak about what had happened to Wells, and rumor has it that she finally replied blandly, "Well, I really don't know."[278] Stories of Wells's suicide were published in multiple cities around the country, and each had their own spin on his reasons for making such a drastic choice. Only one, small Colorado paper, the *Eagle Valley Enterprise*, dared to implicate Hill in Wells's demise (by mentioning a female he scorned)—no other paper hinted at the possibility of her involvement. Wells's obituary in the *Rocky Mountain News* claimed his suicide was the result of losing all $15 million of Whitney's money.[279]

Presumably, Hill had influence over what was printed regarding her relationship with Bulkeley Wells and his ultimate demise. It is reasonable to assume that she would not have wanted details of her involvement with him broadcasted locally or nationally, as such a scandal could have tarnished her reputation as Denver's society leader. If an individual was party to a publicly covered scandal, it was said that they were forbidden from some aristocratic courts in Europe. It is also highly likely that she played a much smaller role in his demise than local rumors have suggested through the ensuing decades. It seems rather certain that, after Wells's elopement, he was excluded from Denver's high society and many of his connections within that circle. Wells did lose money for the Whitneys; that fact, partnered with his gambling addiction and the beginning of the Great Depression, presumably also factored into his financial troubles. Regardless, Wells's social and economic ruin and his eventual suicide displayed, once again, the high stakes game that was Louise Hill's fashionable society.

While Louise Hill never flaunted her affair with Bulkeley Wells, she never made an effort to hide it either. Members of the press were well aware of the affair as it was happening, as were the other individuals in her social circle. Her actions regarding her affair clearly showed that she was a woman in transition; she had a desire to live a fully modern lifestyle, but she did not want to isolate herself entirely from the morality of the high society past. She kept some things out of the public eye, which really displayed her intermediary position between Victorian gentility and modern society. Though her refusal to address the affair in the papers may have seemed contradictory to her embrace of her sexuality as a modern woman, she was actually acting in a contemporary capacity by taking place in the affair and being comfortable enough to not hide her actions from fashionable society or the press.

6

DENVER'S DAZZLING DOYENNE

While Hill did find great success in the Denver community at the beginning of her societal reign, she was not nationally or internationally recognized as a modern society queen. Hill sought to be acknowledged as the Mrs. Astor of the west, and she used her intelligence, tenacity and wealth to help make the leap into the international smart set. With lofty goals of associating with royalty, Hill used her connections to achieve her desires. In an undated newspaper article from the Louise Hill collection scrapbook, the author wrote that Mrs. Hill was "not exactly being presented at the court of St. James," but she was "hobnobbing with the next-door neighbor to royalty." She joined her close friends the Thomas F. Walsh family in Paris, and "being intimate with the Walsh family on the other side of the water," the columnist insinuated, "[was] awfully close to the Belgian throne." The reporter concluded the article by foreshadowing Mrs. Hill's future and stated, "The social aspirations of the Hills to mingle with royalty may yet see fulfillment."[280]

Through Hill's international connection with the Walsh family and the assistance of an acquaintance (U.S. ambassador and Mrs. Whitelaw Reid) she had made through her friend Mrs. Avery, a wealthy woman from Colorado Springs, she was able to achieve her ultimate desire. Mrs. Avery was acquainted with Mrs. Stuyvesant "Mamie" Fish, who was considered a notable society woman in both New York and Newport, Rhode Island. Later, after the passing of Caroline Astor, "Mamie" Fish was considered to be her successor.

Louise Hill remained connected with the Fish family in the decades following their initial meeting and her English court presentation. In 1935, she threw a party for Hamilton Fish III, the nephew of Mamie Fish, when he visited Denver. *From left to right*: Mr. Phipps, Louise Hill, Hamilton Fish III and Mrs. Hodges. The group is pictured here at the 1935 dinner that was thrown by Louise Hill at her home, where she introduced Congressman Hamilton Fish of New York to Denver society. *Courtesy of the Denver Public Library, Western History Collection, F22465.*

Presumably, Avery mentioned Hill to Fish, and when Hill traveled through New York, she was able to meet Mamie Fish with Mrs. Avery at Fish's home. That meeting opened the door for Louise Hill to make her international societal debut. In an article titled "Denver Society Woman to Enter Palace, Mrs. Crawford Hill Will Be 'Presented,'" a journalist described the event that marked Hill's place in history as the first Denverite to be presented in English court. The article stated:

> *The importance of being presented at court may be judged correctly only when you consider a society woman from any of the lesser cities of America is absolutely unknown outside of her own home. She has no acquaintance worth speaking of among New York's "400," and in the capitals of Europe, there is for her no possibility of recognition. But let her be presented at court, and her whole social status is changed.*[281]

This article provided direct information that was relevant to the comparison of New York City's social scene with Denver's. Without the influence of Mrs. Fish, it would have been nearly impossible for Hill to make her international debut so easily and gracefully. The article clearly states the importance of Hill being accepted by Mrs. Astor or those in her close circle of four hundred. Hill's presentation in the English court "before a brilliant gathering of bedecked and bedowered [*sic*] nobility" was her first step in garnering that acceptance. The fact that Hill was going to be presented in England put her, and her 36, in the limelight. It allowed the important individuals in New York to acknowledge Denver as a relevant, elite society. As the article stated, it gave "distinction and [laid] a foundation for the future recognition of Denver society."[282]

Many of the local newspapers covered Hill's presentation story. The *Denver Republican* published an article that described Hill's exquisite presentation dress. The journalist wrote that Hill "attracted much attention in a particularly handsome gown of white satin, embroidered with diamonds, with a comb train of red velvet, heavily brocaded with gold."[283] The author continued their description by stating her "ornaments were a pearl and diamond collar with lace, a string of pearls and a tiara of diamonds with pear-shaped pearls."[284] During her presentation, Hill was received by the Prince and Princess of Wales and the Duke of Connaught.

Louise Hill's exquisite presentation train, photographed here in 2017, was made of red velvet and heavily brocaded with gold. Although her gown has been lost to the ravages of time, her train lives on, thanks to the preservation efforts of History Colorado. *Photograph courtesy of Shelby Carr; collections item property of History Colorado, #H.6047.1.*

Louise Hill in her gown crafted for presentation to King Edward VII at the Court of St. James, London. *Courtesy of History Colorado, Accession #90.314.28.*

After her presentation at court, the notoriety and popularity of the 36 only continued to grow, as did her features in the society pages. From that point forward, Hill was acquainted with numerous members of Europe's nobility, including lords, ladies and Princess and Prince Henry XXXIII of Reuss, a former principality in what is now East Germany.[285] She was also the only woman in Denver permitted to socially entertain President William Howard Taft during his 1911 trip to Denver; she even had an addition built on the south-facing area of her home for his visit.[286] Hill "added one more leaf to her diplomatic chaplet" when she lunched with Li Yung Yew—the imperial Chinese consul general of San Francisco—at her former Cleveland Place residence (which Dr. T. Foo Yuen, a Chinese herb doctor, was renting from her at the time).[287] After the exclusive luncheon that "all society yearned" to attend, Hill was praised for her grace and ease that allowed her to be as familiar with the "etiquette of the Manchu dynasty" as she was with the Sacred 36. A newspaper column even stated that no diplomats visited Denver without meeting Mrs. Hill, who was as well versed in entertaining that set as a "scientist with his indefatigable net."[288]

Hill's national and international presence was cemented further in 1909, when Elizabeth Gordon, the head editor of *Harper's Bazaar*, sent Hill a letter requesting she write an article for the magazine. Gordon stated that, at the request of the magazine's president, Colonel George Harvey, she wrote to inquire if Hill would "represent Denver" by writing an article for the *Bazaar* on the subject of "Western versus Eastern society." Gordon enclosed an article written by Lady Randolph Churchill on London society as well as a piece composed by Mrs. Julia Ward Howe on Boston society in order for Hill to get an idea for "the kind of material [they desired]."[289] In May 1910, Hill's article, entitled "East vs. West," was published in *Harper's Bazaar*, and in it, Hill tackled many myths about the West and attempted to present Denver as a relevant, cultural city with a bustling society to the broad readership of the *Bazaar*. Hill stated that, though previous issues of the *Bazaar* had included pieces on great Eastern cities, her piece on "'Social Denver' would be an impossible subject" to the readers' minds, as she felt, to them, "no such place exists." Hill stated that so many individuals still looked at Denver as the "wild west," where people lived "in the most primitive way," with "stray Indians walking about" and the "occasional herd of buffalo roaming through [the] streets." Denver, she wrote, was a "civilized cosmopolitan city" that lay "proudly in the dazzling sunshine beneath the deep blue Colorado sky." She continued, stating that, in order to understand the social conditions she had created in Colorado, one "must remember Denver's extreme youth." Denver occupied a unique space in that, while it was situated in the western part of the United States, it was "entirely composed of Eastern people," socially speaking. Hill's article clearly represents her position and motivation for elevating Denver from its pioneer roots and misconceptions to that of a cultured city worth international recognition. It also speaks to her attempts to connect to the East while distinguishing herself and her society as holding a unique place in the national social scene.

A minor indiscretion tarnished Hill's social record. On September 19, 1919, Crawford Hill sent a letter to George W. Gano Esquire, the president of the Denver Country Club. The letter, penned by Bulkeley Wells for Crawford—further showing how complex the relationship was between Wells and the Hills—stated that Louise Hill had received correspondence from the board of directors of the club "advising her that the board had suspended her for a period of sixty days on the grounds that she had violated the rules and bylaws of the club, with respect to an incident which occurred in the club on the evening of August 9."[290] Crawford and Bulkeley's letter also went on to state that Mrs. Hill was only an "associate member" of the club through his membership, and therefore, the "provisions of Article X of the bylaws" were only applicable to the male members of the club.[291] Furthermore, Crawford noted that Mrs. Hill had attempted to reply to the complaint in writing, but her letter was perhaps too strongly worded, as she had to change sentences and expressions before she could mail the letter. Finally, Hill wrote that his wife did not "desire to involve anyone else in this matter, nor to evade responsibility for her action," though it is possible that she did and did not want a scandal on her hands. She left town immediately and traveled to Memphis—perhaps until the incident blew over.[292]

This handwritten note from Bulkeley Wells to Crawford Hill explains that he composed a letter on his behalf to the president of the Denver Country Club and enclosed two copies of it for Hill to review. It currently resides with a copy of the typewritten letter in the Louise Hill Collection at History Colorado. *Courtesy of History Colorado, MSS 309 Louise Hill personal correspondence.*

The incident that Hill was referring to was not discussed further in his collection of letters. Based on the rules and bylaws of the Denver Country Club at the time, there are a few strong possibilities as to what the incident may have been. One rule of the club was that the "privilege of occupying rooms at the club house" was restricted to men.[293] It is possible that another member of the club found Mrs. Hill occupying a room upstairs to meet her lover, Bulkeley Wells, as they were known to disappear during club events. Another rule of the club was that "no alcoholic liquor shall be brought, distributed or consumed within the club house or on the club grounds."[294] Louise Hill was well known for her champagne luncheons, cocktail parties and for providing liquor for other people's parties.[295] It is highly likely that, during Prohibition, she still would have wanted to drink alcohol at social events; perhaps someone caught her drinking on club grounds. The most likely occurrence, however, was discussed in Bonniwell and Halaas's book, *The History of the Denver Country Club.* In their work, the authors mentioned that, on the evening of August 9, 1919, Mrs. Hill visited the club with a young male acquaintance named Julian Welles. As previously mentioned, Hill was a pioneer in implementing rather suggestive animal dances in Denver—a practice that the Denver Country Club was not fond of. When she arrived at the club on August 9, she found a notice from the club's board warning against "lewd" dancing. Hill supposedly snatched the notice from the wall and "proceeded to dance the 'shimmy'" with Welles.[296]

On August 21, the board shared its thoughts on Mrs. Hill's actions by posting an edict that stated:

> *ORDERED, that notice in writing be given by the secretary to Mrs. Crawford Hill of the complaint and charges presented by the house committee, containing a specification thereof, and advising her that the board of directors will, at a meeting of such directors to be held at the club house, on the night of September 8, 1919, proceed to consider such complaint and charges and that it will, at the same time, consider and statement or defense with respect to such complaint and charges as Mrs. Hill may wish to submit in writing in the meantime.*[297]

Though she was an advocate for a contemporary society, Hill needed to be careful, at times, of how far she pushed the boundaries. A society editor of the time noted, "Mrs. Hill may be counted on to do a thing when she believes it is for the right," and while she risked her reputation countless times by trying to establish new cultural traditions, a scandal could have had serious repercussions for her role in society.[298] The stakes of her society game were always high; one major misstep could have meant a tumble down the social ladder. This incident also showed that, while Hill was attempting to be a modern woman, she could not always escape long-established genteel requirements.

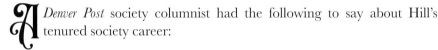

7

THE END OF AN ERA AND DENVER'S DOWAGER QUEEN

A *Denver Post* society columnist had the following to say about Hill's tenured society career:

> *Mrs. Hill's supremacy dates back to the days when she fell heir to the position of her mother-in-law....In Colorado, of a certainty, she stands alone in the realm of social achievement, and her prowess extends beyond the boundaries of the West. When Mrs. Hill goes to New York, she is sought out by leaders in Knickerbocker society, her presence in London is not unheralded, in Paris she is a figure in the American colony, while at Newport, her friends are legion....To be a leader requires a special kind of genius, and Mrs. Hill evidently has it.*[299]

Hill's reign over high society and her national and international travel continued through the 1920s and 1930s. Her favorite destinations were Memphis, Newport, New York, London and Paris. She entertained presidents and fabulously wealthy and titled society people. She never told anyone her age, and newspaper reporters stated she still entertained in her sixties with the exuberance she had in her thirties. Hill once stated that she "was born in North Carolina, where a girl becomes sixteen when she's about twelve or fourteen. She stays sixteen until she's twenty-one, and she remains twenty-one until she's thirty. Finally, she's eighty-five, and then she tells everyone she's one hundred."[300] Wherever Mrs. Hill traveled, newspapers reported that things "looked up," for "wherever Mrs. Hill goes, she is not only a very welcome guest, but she is the center."[301]

By 1942, Hill had shut down her mansion for parties and social gatherings, due to the ravages of World War II. In Hill's later years, the upkeep of her large mansion became too much for her, the war's pressures made keeping servants difficult and she suffered from a stroke around 1947. Consequently, she and her staff moved into the Skyline Apartments at the Brown Palace (room 904), and her sons sold her mansion to the newly established Jewish Town Club.[302] That same year, many of Hill's expensive clothes and furnishings were put up for auction. Six hundred items were appraised at $16,000 and went up for sale. All of the available items were displayed for two days prior to the auction, and many of the home's furnishings went for far less than they appraised, and the most expensive item was a French commode that sold for $750. Hill's English court presentation ensemble was received with "ooh and ahs" from the crowd. The lavish gown was sold for $22.50.[303] Another piece of social importance was auctioned off that day as well: the life-sized figure of a nude woman holding a bouquet of Easter lilies, Mrs. Hill's favorite flower. The statue was a staple of the home. Every year, Louise Hill would carefully keep it covered until the warm spring weather emerged—it signaled the beginning of a new social season. The Town Club was able to purchase it at the auction for $10. Members of the Hill family also retained a few pieces from the mansion, including the furniture that was in the bedroom where William Howard Taft stayed during his visit. Frances Melrose, a *Rocky Mountain News* reporter, noted that, at the conclusion of the auction, with the removal of the Hill furnishings and the "transfiguration of the famous old mansion," another piece of "pioneer Denver [had] passed into oblivion."[304]

Hill became a bit of a recluse in her later years and was saddened by the lack of visits from her sons and their families. She wrote to her niece, in 1938, that she felt her own letters were "so stupid, so that I am sure that they bother you."[305] She also wrote to Nathaniel and Crawford in 1940 that she knew they had only "slight interest in how [she was] doing but... you might feel sorry for me, as I have been so terribly sick suffering from intense pain, confined to my bed constantly."[306] She wrote both of her sons again that year and stated she had spent "so much time trying to convince you not to come out here as it would bore you to death....But I did think you could send me a postcard."[307]

She spent the remaining years of her life in her Brown Palace apartment and died there of pneumonia in 1955, at the age of ninety-two, leaving an estate worth just over $5 million.[308] Perhaps in a nod to her childhood house

Mrs. Hill's backyard statue—a nude woman holding a bouquet of Easter lilies, Mrs. Hill's favorite flower—signaled the beginning of spring and the next year's social season. *Courtesy of the Denver Public Library, Western History Collection, X-26654.*

Louise Hill, seen here exiting the Brown Palace, began living on the ninth floor of the hotel (designated the Skyline Apartments) after her Sherman Street mansion became too much for her to maintain. *Courtesy of the Denver Public Library, Western History Collection, Rh-648.*

of worship, her funeral was held at an institution bearing the same name, St. John's Episcopal, in Denver. She was survived by her two sons, Nathaniel P. of New York and Crawford Jr. of Newport; her four grandchildren; and seven great-grandchildren. Both of her sons died shortly after her. Crawford Jr. passed in 1960, in Palm Beach, Florida, and Nathaniel died in 1965, in Boston, Massachusetts.[309]

Hill led, by high society terms, a fabulous life. She was a tough mother to her sons (she once wrote a letter to Crawford stating, "The Boettchers… said that you were so fat they would never have known you had someone at the table not told them who you were.…I told you about growing fat…. Get thin and stand up."), but she also loved them fiercely.[310] Noted in the papers for her sensational personality, Hill also appeared to possess an insatiable thirst for wealth, a love of honors and a public recognition of her power and success. Local newspapers praised her beauty and aided in perpetuating her image of unattainable perfection. An untitled article described the situation perfectly when the columnist reported that, at a Denver Club ball, "all eyes watched for the social leader, as if, instead of

Louise Hill, pictured here with her sons, Nathaniel and Crawford, when they were young children, was a tough mother, but she loved her sons fiercely throughout her lifetime. *Courtesy of the Denver Public Library, Western History Collection, F23307.*

meeting the queen, she were really the queen herself."[311] As the leader of the "whipped cream" of Denver society, Hill was well known for setting the social mores of the Mile-High City and could "topple an individual from the social ladder or raise him to the heights."[312] When she was asked by a society reporter from the *Rocky Mountain News* about what inherent qualities one must have to be a social leader, Hill supposedly replied, "First, you must have money. Then, you must have the knowledge to give people a wonderful time." The reporter added that Mrs. Hill, indeed, "had those ingredients and used them well."[313]

Though tragedy signaled the beginning of her life and despair fraught the end of it, Louise Sneed Hill strived to consistently display her genteel breeding and poise. Defined by local papers as an animated conversationalist and a thorough sophisticate, Denver society's dowager queen was a force to be reckoned with; her high society contest carried high risks, and individuals who dared enter the arena had to be constantly alert and mind their steps. For Hill, high risk resulted in high reward, as she effectively put the Mile-High City on the map. Her success as the "ruling queen" of society was a "well-ordered existence in which intelligence, affability and diplomacy [were] the ruling planets....An uncanny vision and never-say-die spirit [also] played important parts."[314] With Denver's vastly different population and geography, Louise Hill had to work from the bottom up to modernize the culture of the hub of the pioneer West in order to create an aristocratic-style society and usher in a contemporary era.

Hill pushed the boundaries of what was appropriate. She paid no attention as members of the old guard "raised their eyebrows" at her modern choices, including her parties, where "wine and mixed drinks were served freely, instead of the usual teas; the champagne was more bubbly, and no one was asked to leave when the clock struck midnight."[315] As a southerner, Hill did not have the same suspicion of leisure that others had in the puritanical North. Though she consistently aligned herself in interviews with the Puritan ideal of working hard, she made every effort, especially in her later years, to distinguish her leisure as hard work. In an interview with newspaper reporter Mildred Morris, Hill defended the role of a high society leader as just that. Many times, she compared the work of society women to the work of individuals in the armed forces. She felt the "training the society woman receives on the social battlefield [was] as excellent as the training of a soldier," because oftentimes, society women were "called upon to lead movements important to the community." She

Above: Crawford Jr. (*left*) and Nathaniel P. IV (*right*) were both well-educated and successful men. They passed shortly after their mother, in 1960 and 1965, respectively. *Courtesy of History Colorado, accession #90.314.368 and #90.314.37.*

Left: Louise Hill strived to rule society with dignity and poise until the end of her life. *Courtesy of History Colorado, accession #90.314.332.*

admitted that society leaders had "the leisure other women lack," but they were also "doing really big things in the world." They were "trained to be alert, to be interested in the big vital problems and, above all, to be thoughtful of others."[316]

115

Hill continually distinguished her leisure as productive work and felt it was important to continue to push herself to accomplish new feats. "You think I am all for vanity and frivols," she once said to a newspaper reporter while leading them through her home to her sunroom, where she proudly displayed a "gleaming white figure and inspirational face in marble." The head and shoulders of the *Lady of the Lilies* was modeled by Hill herself. She told the newspaper reporter that she would "love to make this sort of thing my work…to have a studio of my own in which I might find out just what my talent for sculpture amounts to. I am simply yearning to find out if I could pay my own way if I were turned adrift." Per her modern mind-set, Hill had a great deal of respect for women who worked in disciplines outside of high society, and she once stated that if she "had ever envied anyone it [was] the woman who [had] tested her gift and ability to stand free of the family prop."[317] She was even publicly criticized by members of high society for entertaining women who worked. One high-society woman told the press it was "perfectly absurd for Mrs. Hill to entertain at luncheon and tea some of the young women in town who work for a living."

Hill paid no attention to the criticism and was defended by newspaper reporters for her progressive ideas. Society columnist Leola Allard defended Hill and wrote a piece in direct response to the incident. She wrote that Mrs. Hill was the "most human woman that ever drew breath." The reporter continued, "if anyone interests her, she takes the liberty, if you please, of having them in her own home.…She doesn't ask them to drink their tea with those who don't approve of working for a living, but she enjoys them and has the tact to invite them with only those who are their friends."[318] This kindness from Hill extended even further, to those who worked for the press. *Rocky Mountain News* photographer Harry Mellon Rhoads knew Mrs. Hill for the entirety of his life. When Rhoads was temporarily blinded with flash powder while taking photos at a Denver Club party, Hill made sure to visit him every day for two weeks, and she hired specialists and private nurses to care for him. A *Rocky Mountain News* article also recounted a time when an unnamed society editor fell ill, and Hill moved her into her Sherman Street home.[319]

Hill was very good to those who worked for her as well—she treated them as if they were members of her own family—which made for loyal employees who aided her success. One of her most tenured staff members, Cora Cowan, passed away in 1930, and when Nina Price, Hill's "second girl" (not her personal maid), was in her seventies, she remembered that Hill had "moments of grief" over Cowan's death. Cowan, an Ohio native, worked

This image of Louise Hill during her mid-life was taken by her close friend and *Rocky Mountain News* photographer Harry Mellon Rhoades around 1910. *Courtesy of the Denver Public Library, Western History Collection, Rh-5816.*

in the Hill household for twenty-eight years, according to her obituary, and was well known in Denver. She was charged as the nurse of Hill's sons from birth and served in other various capacities in the Hill household throughout her career there. She was noted as being indispensable to Mrs. Hill. A 1913 newspaper article titled "Mrs. Hill Fined as Smuggler" told the amusing story of Hill and Cowan as "partners in crime" apparently "smuggling gowns" back from Europe. Hill and Cowan had supposedly cut the foreign labels out of recently purchased clothing and replaced them with American labels. No arrests were made, though Hill plead guilty and paid a fine of $300.[320] In 1916, Cowan fell ill with appendicitis, and it was Louise Hill that sat by her hospital bed and helped nurse her back to health. When Hill, who was then in New York preparing to sail to Europe, received word of Cowan's death, she immediately changed her plans and traveled back to Denver with her son Nathaniel. Hill held Cowan's funeral in her home on Sherman Street. Price recalled Hill crying years after Cowan's passing; her heart ached with sadness, still missing her years later.[321]

She was not only a friend to women who worked, but she was also a friend to those who were fighting for women's rights. Throughout the national push for women's suffrage, Hill held events for the cause at her home and participated in "Denver's Longest Parade." The parade, which was comprised of more than three thousand women, started at the congressional union (a suffrage organization) and was grand marshalled by a woman. Hill rode at the head of the parade with her sister-in-law Mrs. Lucius Cuthbert and her close friends Mrs. P. Randolph Morris and Mrs. Horton Pope.[322] In 1916, Hill was even named as a potential candidate to serve as a delegate for the Chicago Republican National Convention in the hopes of "[re-establishing] the cause [of women's enfranchisement] in non-suffrage and anti-suffrage states."[323]

Though she felt work was important—and that women who worked served a great purpose in society—she believed the world needed entertainment in addition to work and contended that "those who supply the entertainment are as useful as those who do the work." She felt that thinking up "new entertainment before the old [began] to bore" was no simple task but one that "required not only energy but brains." Hill also asserted the society woman who sat "around in satins and diamonds and [rose] at noon" only existed "in the paperback novels." As a society leader, she was always awake at 8:00 a.m., regardless of how late she was out the night before, as she always had to read the morning paper in order to be "well versed on all current topics." She had to be able to discuss anything and everything, from "the Irish question to the Mexican situation, with equal facility," for there was "no telling what [her] dinner partner [would] be interested in, and [she] must not be a bore."[324]

Louise Hill—through her perseverance, morals, manner, charm, ideals and bribery—was able to push society toward a modern way of thinking and accomplish her goals. She attained camaraderie with the socialites of New York City, the society at the top of the social strata during her lifetime. Due to her great wealth and determination to put her city on the map (and secure her title as a society noble), Hill influenced the minds of Denver citizens every day. She employed feature articles in newspaper publications that relentlessly displayed her cultural capital and her new ideas of gentility.

The Sacred 36—a group the April 22, 1934 *News* society pages pegged as "more difficult to crash than the confines of Buckingham Palace"— represented the first iteration of an elite social scene in Denver and gained the city worldwide acknowledgment as a legitimate cultural and educated place. Hill's creation of an aristocratic social scene in pioneer Colorado forever altered the epicenter of the pioneer Rocky Mountain West. By deriving her tactics from Mrs. Caroline Astor, Hill managed to turn the "social wasteland" of Denver into a highly intellectual and cultured society that was recognized and respected internationally. In the words of those who lived during her reign, Mrs. Crawford Hill was an "institution"; she had "a wit, was intelligent, and would say just the right thing that was surprising and on the mark."[325] She was said to have "mastered the art of making people feel more than they really were. Anybody who ever met Mrs. Hill left her feeling enriched in some spiritual fashion. And she turned on the same charm and wit for the postman as well as her honored guest."[326]

Hill was a revolutionary spirit during a transitional time, when American society began looking toward the future. She was an agent of change and advocated for the acceptance of leisure as work and not simply for leisure's sake. In a time when Victorian culture was suspicious of luxury and leisure, she emphasized the labor of her efforts to appease the masses and ease the transition into a contemporary school of thought. By putting an emphasis on amusement and an independent identity for women, Hill was a trailblazer who helped usher in the phenomena of mass and celebrity culture. By using the press to pull back the veil on high society, she allowed the rest of the class system to indulge in the drama of the bourgeoisie. She presented herself as the foremost authority on all things fun and fashionable in the press and created intimate relationships with those writing about her.

Louise (*seated*) was acquainted with actress, hostess and interior decorator Elsie de Wolfe (*standing*). De Wolfe, also known by her married name, Lady Mendl, was recognized for her "innovative and anti-Victorian interiors." *Courtesy of the Denver Public Library, Western History Collection, F11584.*

Louise Hill led, by high-society terms, a fabulous life. Pictured here in her later years, Louise was a trailblazer who helped usher in the phenomena of mass and celebrity culture. She defined high society for Denver during the Gilded Age, and with the end of her life, as American society began to worship Hollywood actors as celebrities, came the end of an era in which the fashionably wealthy reigned supreme. *Courtesy of the Denver Public Library, Western History Collection, F22470.*

Women like Louise Hill have been written out of the narrative, grossly misrepresented or ended up as merely a chapter or a footnote in American history. These women were high-society leaders and so much more; they were also philanthropists, preservationists and advocates of change who held themselves to high standards of genteel breeding and accomplished amazing feats. It is hard to imagine what the city of Denver would be like today if not for the influence of the tiny but powerful Louise Sneed Hill.

EPILOGUE

Upon Louise Sneed Hill's death, *Rocky Mountain News* reporter Pasquale Marranzino wrote that, to those who knew her, Mrs. Hill was a "social artist," and when first making her acquaintance, they immediately knew she "had the makings to take the reins of Denver society….She took on a studied life and built it to perfection." He went on to state that Mrs. Hill led Denver society "as it [had] never been governed before or since.…[She] appeared to have more effect on Denver than any other woman who ever lived [there]. And it seems important that someone should assay that importance and give Mrs. Hill her proper place in history." Unfortunately, despite a valiant effort on Mr. Marranzino's part, this has not previously been the case. In fact, it has been quite the opposite.

Throughout my research, I encountered a great deal of incorrect information about Hill's life. I hope that this book will enlighten individuals on who the misunderstood Louise Hill really was. A major goal of my work was to debunk all of the myths depicted in the *Unsinkable Molly Brown* motion picture. In that film, though Hill's name is never used, she is represented by the character Mrs. Gladys McGraw, the acknowledged leader of Denver society who lived on Pennsylvania Avenue and who gave a party when her roses bloomed. The movie claimed that Hill (McGraw) did not make contributions to charitable organizations, was snobbish (didn't accept people unlike her, even though they donated so much to others), shunned Brown and had to be taught by Brown how to properly curtsy and address foreign dignitaries.

Louise's favorite portrait of herself, which hung in her Sherman Street mansion. *Courtesy of History Colorado, accession #2000.129.1418.*

As I was conducting my research, I stumbled across an article in the Colorado Encyclopedia that made quick mention of Mrs. Crawford Hill. At the very end of the article, it stated that Margaret "Molly" Brown would be remembered long after Louise Hill would be forgotten. Though I was already inspired to make this book a reality, that quote in particular lit a fire in me to push through and complete the project to the best of my ability.

With this work, I hope to change the previously existing narrative of the life of Louise Hill and address the question: Was she the "snobbiest woman in Denver" and the mythical dowager queen that individuals believe her to have been, or was she actually a modern, forward-thinker? I believe that she possessed traits of both—she was a tough society queen who ruled with formed guidelines, but she infused modern ideas to craft an entirely new society. She intended to elevate the level of Denver on an international scale. While Hill was not without her faults, she achieved impressive feats and revolutionized the Denver social scene at the turn of the twentieth century.

NOTES

Introduction

1. Eastom, "Hospitality of Mrs. Hill World Famed."
2. History Colorado Center, untitled article, undated, Louise Hill Scrapbook, Carton 35, Stephen H. Hart Library and Research Center.
3. Morris, "Society Defended by Mrs. Hill," 5.
4. "Sacred Thirty-Six," *Rocky Mountain News*.
5. Bibby, "Making the American Aristocracy."
6. M. Rockwell, "Gender Transformations."
7. May, *Screening Out the Past*.
8. Ibid., 6
9. Ibid., 107

Chapter 1

10. Bethell, "July 27th Sunday."
11. History Colorado Center, "Society Forecasts," undated, Louise Hill Scrapbook, carton 35, Stephen H. Hart Library and Research Center.
12. NCGenweb Project and North Carolina, "Sneed Plantation."
13. Peace, *"Zeb's Black Baby."*
14. Pace, interview.
15. Ancestry, "Marriage bond Louisa Bethel and William Morgan Sneed."

16. "Deaths,"*Raleigh Register*.
17. St. John's Episcopal Church, "Pamphlet."
18. Gresham, *Biographical Cyclopedia*, 164. A theory also circulates that Sneed served under a supposed cousin of Daniel Morgan named William Morgan and that he named his first child after his former leader. William Morgan is a name that continued to follow the generations of Sneeds to come.
19. Ancestry.com, Marriage Bond Louisa Bethel and William Morgan Sneed 28 June 1842, North Carolina, Marriage Index, 1741–2004; NCGenweb Project, "Sneed Plantation."
20. North Carolina County Register of Deeds, Microfilm, Record Group 048, North Carolina State Archives, Raleigh, NC.
21. Historic American Buildings Survey, creator, Samuel Henderson, Richard Henderson, Archibald Henderson, Richard Bullock, Adolphus Eugene White and Henry White, sponsor North Carolina State College and Eugene Wilson Brown, *Ashland Plantation House, Satterwhite Road, Henderson, Vance County, NC*, Henderson North Carolina Vance County, 1933, documentation compiled after, photograph, www.loc.gov.
22. Peace, *"Zeb's Black Baby."*
23. Williams, "Transylvania Company."
24. Fowles and Toules, "Col. Richard Henderson," 37–45.
25. Gresham, *Biographical Cyclopedia*, 164.
26. Correspondence from Crawford Hill to James A. Rose, Esq., dated March 27, 1900, Crawford Hill Collection, vol. 1, Western History Genealogy Department, Denver Public Library.
27. "Daughter," *Tarborough Southerner*.
28. "Letter to the Editor," *Tribune*.
29. Lee, *Winnie Davis*.
30. "Mrs. Davis Relative Mrs. Crawford Hill," *Rocky Mountain News*.
31. Morris, "Society Defended by Mrs. Hill," 5.
32. Ibid.
33. Military History Online, "William Morgan Sneed."
34. National Archives, Records of the commissary general of prisoners, record group 249, selected records of the War Department relating to Confederate prisoners of war, 1861–65 (National Archives microfilm publication M598, 145 rolls), Washington, D.C., 434.
35. Ancestry, "Marriages of Granville County."
36. Peace, *"Zeb's Black Baby,"* 215–8.
37. "Latest News," *Raleigh North Carolina Semi-Weekly News*; *Raleigh North Carolina Semi-Weekly News*, October 9, 1864.

38. Peace, "*Zeb's Black Baby,*" 216–18

39. Ibid.

40. "Death of Mrs. S.A. Sneed," *Torch Light.*

41. University of North Carolina at Chapel Hill, subseries 6.1. parochial visits, 1870–99, in the Pettigrew family papers no. 592, Southern Historical Collection, Wilson Library.

42. *Daily Dispatch,* September 1931.

43. University of North Carolina at Chapel Hill, vol. 2, Diary, 1890–93, in the Goodrich Wilson Marrow papers, no. 1723, Southern Historical Collection, Wilson Library.

44. "Traveling Around," *Oxford Public Ledger.*

45. "Social and Personal," *Henderson Gold Leaf.*

46. Leonard, *Woman's Who's Who of America.*

47. Anonymous, "St. Mary's School," 459.

48. "Law Firm," *Memphis Daily Appeal;* "Memphis Lawyer," *New York Times.*

49. "At the Altar," *Inter Ocean.*

50. "Mont Eagle Springs," *Memphis Daily Appeal.*

51. "Personal Points," *Richmond Dispatch.*

52. White, *Republic for Which It Stands,* 12. Kennedy continued in his introduction, stating that, after the end of the war, the "standard usage" gradually became "the United States is" singular and unified.

53. Ibid., 17.

54. Ibid.

55. McPherson, *Battle Cry of Freedom,* preface, 859.

56. White, *Republic for Which It Stands,* 16.

57. Mark Twain and Charles Dudley Warner, *The Gilded Age* (Hartford, CT: American Pub. Co., 1873).

58. White, *Republic for Which It Stands,* 17.

59. DuBois, *Black Reconstruction in America,* 708. In this statement, DuBois was referring to reconstruction as a whole, but he also called it an "attempt to make black men American citizens," further evoking the racial tensions that came out of the periods of Reconstruction and the Gilded Age.

60. Richardson, *West from Appomattox,* 7. Richardson also stated that an active government was desired to benefit the "general interest," as "middle class women and their husbands began to call for government activism to defend the individualist household, the center, as they saw it, of American society" (Richardson, *West from Appomattox,* 217). Karen Halttunen noted in *Confidence Men and Painted Women* that middle class Americans constituted the "best society in the land" (95).

61. Richardson, *West from Appomattox*, 7

62. White, *Republic for Which It Stands*, 171.

63. Ibid.

64. Ibid.

65. Though Edward L. Ayers noted in *The Promise of the New South* that the segregation in the post–Civil War era "did not spread inexorably and evenly across the face of the South," he stated that while "most whites seem to have welcomed segregation in general, others saw no need to complicate the business of everyday life with additional distinctions between the races," (137) Heather Cox Richardson noted in *West from Appomattox* that Republicans believed agriculture was the "prime factor of economic growth" and, in turn, passed the Homestead Act in 1862 (25). While this act was intended to benefit those hoping to achieve the American vision of a free labor society, in order to settle these lands and travel to them, they had to once again displace Native Americans. Eric Foner stated in *A Short History of Reconstruction* that the vision of an agricultural nation was really only possible in the west as the South suffered an "economic disaster" during the Civil War that rendered it rather useless in terms of agricultural success (55).

66. Trachtenberg, *Incorporation of America*, 5.

67. Fink, *Long Gilded Age*, 18.

68. Richardson, *West from Appomattox*, 67.

69. Ibid., 7. This middle-class "vision," as Richardson noted, also "limited women's role in society by basing their power on positions as wives and mothers, not as independent, equal individuals."

70. White, *Republic for Which It Stands*, 941.

71. Ibid, 20.

72. Ibid. White went on to discuss the home in terms of race and ethnicity, stating that "those who failed to secure proper homes were cast as a danger to the white home—as happened to Chinese, blacks, Indians…and some European immigrants."

73. Ibid.

74. Ibid., 22. White discussed the "great age of the Midwest" that also occurred from Abraham Lincoln's time through the Gilded Age.

75. Ibid., 34.

76. Cashman, *America in the Gilded Age*, 3–4

77. White, *It's Your Misfortune and None of My Own*, 3–4.

78. Papers of Pickney C. and William D. Bethell, 1848–1901, "Biography of William D. Bethell, 1840–1906," Library of the State Historical Society of Colorado.

79. "Captain Bethel Dies in Denver," *Pueblo Chieftain*.
80. Historic Memphis, "Mayors of Memphis."
81. For more on Captain Bethell, read *Memphis: In Black and White* by Beverly G. Bond and Janann Sherman (Mount Pleasant: Arcadia Publishing, 2003).

Chapter 2

82. Noel, *City and the Saloon*, 78.
83. "Weds a Southern Belle," *Denver Post*.
84. History Colorado Center, "Denver's Most Exclusive Set Ruled by One," undated, Louise Hill Scrapbook, carton 35, Stephen H. Hart Library and Research Center.
85. Hill, "Nathaniel P. Hill Inspects Colorado," 241.
86. Steele, "Honorable Nathaniel Peter Hill," 428.
87. Stone, "Nathaniel Peter Hill," 7.
88. Ibid.; Headley, *History of Orange County*, 381.
89. Stone, "Nathaniel Peter Hill," 7.
90. Steele, "Honorable Nathaniel Peter Hill," 428; Hull, "Hill, Nathaniel Peter."
91. Stone, "Nathaniel Peter Hill," 7; Steele, "Honorable Nathaniel Peter Hill," 428.
92. Fell, *Ores to Metals*, 11; Steele, "Honorable Nathaniel Peter Hill," 428.
93. Fell, *Ores to Metals*, 428.
94. Stone, "Nathaniel Peter Hill," 7; Steele, "Honorable Nathaniel Peter Hill," 428; Mitchell, "Nathaniel P. Hill"; Hull, "Hill, Nathaniel Peter."
95. Appleton, "Hon. Nathaniel P. Hill '56," 77.
96. Fell, *Ores to Metals*, 11.
97. Ibid.
98. Ellen Fisher, Alice Hale Hill Collection Forward, collection 308, Stephen H. Hart Library and Research Center, History Colorado Center.
99. Gibson, *A.J. Gordon*.
100. National Archives and Records Administration (NARA), consolidated lists of Civil War draft registration records (Provost Marshal General's Bureau, consolidated enrollment lists, 1863–1865), record group: 110, collection name: consolidated enrollment lists, 1863–65 (Civil War Union Draft Records), NAI: 4213514, archive volume number: 1 of 3, Washington, D.C.
101. Fell, *Ores to Metals*, 12–8.
102. Ibid., 18; Appleton, "Hon. Nathaniel P. Hill," 77.

103. Hill, "Nathaniel P. Hill Inspects Colorado," 241.

104. Ibid.; Biographical Directory of the United States Congress, "Hill, Nathaniel Peter."

105. Fell, *Ores to Metals*, 25–6.

106. Appleton, "Hon. Nathaniel P. Hill," 77.

107. Fell, "Nathaniel P. Hill," 315–32.

108. Ibid., 331; Biographical Directory of the United States Congress, "Hill, Nathaniel Peter."

109. Biographical Directory of the United States Congress, "Hill, Nathaniel Peter."

110. Fell, *Ores to Metals*, 137.

111. Hill, "Nathaniel P. Hill Inspects Colorado," 241.

112. Biographical Directory of the United States Congress, "Hill, Nathaniel Peter."

113. Appleton, "Hon. Nathaniel P. Hill," 78.

114. Steele, "Honorable Nathaniel Peter Hill," 430.

115. Ibid., 431.

116. Anonymous, "Crawford Hill," 45; *Fourth Estate*, "Prominent Denver Publisher"; Ferril, "Crawford Hill," 280–81.

117. "Around the Tea Table," *Rocky Mountain News*.

118. "Sneed-Hill," *Times Picayune* (New Orleans, LA).

119. "Telegraphic Briefs," *Omaha Bee*.

120. "Crawford Hill Married," *Aspen Daily Times*.

121. History Colorado Center, untitled article, undated, Louise Hill Scrapbook, carton 35, Stephen H. Hart Library and Research Center.

122. History Colorado Center, "Hill-Sneed Wedding," Louise Hill Scrapbook, 1895, carton 35, Stephen H. Hart Library and Research Center.

123. Register of Deaths in the City of Memphis, Tennessee, file no. 49560, 71.

124. "Arrival of Mr. and Mrs. Hill," *Denver Post*.

125. Marilyn Griggs Riley Papers, Louise Hill, manuscript, Box 2, FF32, Western History Genealogy Department, Denver Public Library, 2.

126. Ibid.

127. Jane Haigh, quoted in Limerick, *Ditch in Time*, 48.

128. May, *Screening Out the Past*, 25

129. Bakken and Farrington, *Encyclopedia of Women*, 66–67; Beaton, *Colorado Women*, 50–52.

130. "Mrs. Crawford Hill Fractures Her Wrist," *Denver Post*. Other society articles from the time claim that Hill broke her writs while roller-skating on her roof, not in her ballroom, though this seems to be rather unlikely.

131. Rohe, "Society as a Fine Art."

132. "Colorado Patriots Open Purses," *Denver Post*.

133. Correspondence from A. Piatt Andrews to Louise Hill, dated March 4, 1918, Louise Hill scrapbook, carton 35, Stephen H. Hart Library and Research Center, History Colorado Center.

Chapter 3

134. MacColl and McD. Wallace, *To Marry an English Lord*, 7–10.

135. Rosner, "Portrait of an Unhealthy City."

136. Beckert, *Monied Metropolis*, 18.

137. Matthiessen, *American Renaissance*.

138. Homberger, *Mrs. Astor's New York*, 1, citing Louis Simonin in *Revue des deux mondes, 1874-1875*.

139. Ibid., 262.

140. Wecter, *Saga of American Society*, 333.

141. Homberger, *Mrs. Astor's New York*, preface.

142. Ibid., 25–26.

143. Ibid., 2–6.

144. Wecter, *Saga of American Society*, 289.

145. Ibid.

146. Bibby, "Making the American Aristocracy," 5.

147. Homberger, *Mrs. Astor's New York*, 10.

148. Bushman, *Refinement of Class*, 28–35.

149. Homberger, *Mrs. Astor's New York*, 10.

150. Allen, *Horrible Prettiness*, 144.

151. Eric Homberger discusses this topic at length in his work *Mrs. Astor's New York*. Homberger wrote, "By the 1820s and 1830s, as the revolutionary generation passed from the scene, wealthy people in New York once again bought English goods and looked to London (and Paris) for fashions in dance, music, dress, culture, and social life. New York was the country's cultural and social capital—the individuals of New York City set the trends for the rest of the nation."

152. Bushman, *Refinement of Class in America*, xvii.

153. Ibid., xv.

154. Ibid., xvii.

155. Ibid., xiii.

156. Ibid., 62.

157. Stansell, *City of Women*, 4; Halttunen, *Confidence Men and Painted Women*, 192. Karen Halttunen noted in *Confidence Men and Painted Women* that the "rapid economic and social changes between 1820 and 1850" skewed the formerly accepted notions of social status and personal recognition of place in society.

158. Stansell, *City of Women*, 4.

159. Bushman, *Refinement of Class in America*, xv.

160. Ibid., xv

161. Stansell, *City of Women*, xii.

162. Ibid.

163. Ibid.; May, *Screening Out the Past*, 9; Beckert, *Monied Metropolis*, 75.

164. Stansell, *City of Women*, xii.

165. Ibid.

166. Allen, *Horrible Prettiness*, 146.

167. Rockman, *Scraping By*. There is a great deal more that could be said about social stratification, especially in regard to the working class. Seth Rockman's *Scraping By* discusses unskilled laborers of both genders and various ethnicities. Rockman stated that, for the "workers in [his] book, class experience was waiting…for the harbor to thaw so that low-end jobs might resume…class consciousness was knowing the proper pose of deference to get hired," and "class struggle was trying to meet the rent while scavenging for firewood to stay warm during the winter."

168. Bushman, *Refinement of Class in America*, xiii.

169. Trachtenberg, *Incorporation of America*, 160.

170. Blumin, *Emergence of the Middle Class*. It was in the Jacksonian Era (1829–37) that Stuart Blumin notes in *The Emergence of the Middle Class* that a true middle-class began to emerge. During that time, markets were expanded, and work was structured differently (nonmanual versus manual labor). As the nonmanual labor class began to grow, it formed the defined middle class and asserted that distinction through its manners and fashionable dwellings.

171. Wilentz, *Chants Democratic*, 33. Stansell wrote in *City of Women* that "the employment of immigrants exacerbated the process of sweating and deskilling." Sean Wilentz in his work *Chants Democratic* stated that the "dilution of skill" signified the "mutation of apprenticeship" and the "changing relations" in the "division of labor."

172. Beckert, *Monied Metropolis*, 5.

173. Wecter, *Saga of American Society*.

174. Allen, *Horrible Prettiness*, 34. Larry May, in *Screening Out the Past*, also stated that the elite class, especially those of New York City, "did everything possible to make high level consumption exclusive to their own group, utilizing the fruits of the economy to differentiate themselves from the masses" (35).

175. The rise in the mass consumption of movies and celebrities and the way in which picture houses shaped America (mass consumption's role in remaking class boundaries) is a general theme for Larry May's book *Screening Out the Past*. In this work, he discussed the "moral experimentation" of the twentieth century and the transition of American culture from the Victorian era to that of a modern society.

176. Gordon, *The Great Arizona Orphan Abduction*. Linda Gordon recounts in *The Great Arizona Orphan Abduction* that the white population varied by region. In New York, at the Foundling Hospital, they called the Irish, Polish, and African American populations "comparable categories." Gordon also stated that the concept of race did not classify status as much as "social and economic markings of rank." She wrote that further distinctions were made to classify "upscale German Jews as Germans and Russian Jews as Hebrews." Gordon also touched on the ideas of white workers aligning themselves with their employers rather than their fellow workers due to their different ethnicities.

177. Cashman, *America in the Gilded Age*, 3–4.

178. Trachtenberg, *Incorporation of America*.

179. Beckert, *Monied Metropolis*, 273, 339

180. Ibid., 60.

181. Ibid., 260.

182. MacColl and Wallace, *To Marry an English Lord*, 223.

183. Ibid., 17.

184. Ibid., 17–8.

185. History Colorado Center, "Who are the Mighty Ninety?" undated, Louise Hill Scrapbook, carton 35, Stephen H. Hart Library and Research Center.

186. Rohe, "Society as a Fine Art."

187. Richardson, *West from Appomattox*.

188. West, *Contested Plains*, xviii.

189. "Our Central Gold Region," *Rocky Mountain News*.

190. William Jackson Palmer, quoted in Andrews, *Killing for Coal*, 25.

191. Breger, "Two Replies to Mr. Eilers."

Chapter 4

192. *Oxford Dictionary*, "nouveau riche."
193. Homberger, *Mrs. Astor's New York*, 104.
194. May, *Screening Out the Past*, xiii.
195. Van Rensselaer and Van De Water, *Social Ladder*, 53.
196. Ibid., 22.
197. Hill, "East vs. West," 5.
198. "Babies' Summer Hospital," *Rocky Mountain News*.
199. "Mrs. Brown Climbs Into '36' Crowd," *Denver Post*.
200. Rohe, "Society as a Fine Art."
201. Hill, "East vs. West," 5.
202. White, "Lucius M. Cuthbert"; Kania, *Denver Press Club*; *Rocky Mountain News*, "Sacred Thirty-Six," 7.
203. "Europe Has Fewer Snobs Than America," *Denver Post*, 1–2.
204. Ibid.
205. Hill, "East vs. West," 5.
206. Homberger, *Mrs. Astor's New York*, 8.
207. "Who's Who Social Arc," *Denver Post*.
208. Ibid.
209. *Who's Who in Denver Society*.
210. "Who's Who Social Arc," *Denver Post*.
211. *Who's Who in Denver Society*, 204–7.
212. Scobey, "Anatomy of the Promenade," 203–27.
213. Homberger, *Mrs. Astor's New York*, 6.
214. Ibid., 9.
215. King, *Season of Splendor*, 23.
216. Homberger, *Mrs. Astor's New York*, 125.
217. "Mrs. William Astor's Ball," *New York Times*; "Mrs. Astor's Annual Ball," *New York Times*; "Mrs. Astor's Final Dinner," *New York Times*.
218. Homberger, *Mrs. Astor's New York*, 11–12.
219. Ibid., 266.
220. Iversen, *Molly Brown*, 142.
221. Hill, "East vs. West," 44, 5.
222. Thayer, "Thomas H. Lawrence," 625.
223. "Afternoon Tea," *Rocky Mountain News*.
224. City of Denver Building Permit No. 1071, dated September 5, 1901; City of Denver Building Permit No. 1070, dated August 15, 1902.

225. "Coming Events," *Denver Post*; "Denver Motor Club," *Rocky Mountain News*; "Foo-Wing Herb Co.," *Denver Post*; "Club to Greet Marshall," *Rocky Mountain News*.

226. Renee McReynolds, interviewed by Shelby Carr, personal inquiry, Denver, October 19, 2017.

227. History Colorado Center, untitled newspaper article, undated, Louise Hill Scrapbook, carton 35, Stephen H. Hart Library and Research Center.

228. Ibid.

229. Correspondence from Louise Hill to Mrs. H.H. Tammen, dated March 4, 1927, carton 11, Stephen H. Hart Library and Research Center, History Colorado Center.

230. History Colorado Center, untitled newspaper article, undated, Louise Hill Scrapbook, carton 35, Stephen H. Hart Library and Research Center.

231. Griggs, "Louise Sneed Hill."

232. "Leader of the 'Sacred 36,'" *Historic Denver News*, 7.

233. "Mrs. Hill Helped Crystallize," *Denver Post*.

234. Correspondence from Louise Hill to Miss Helen Eastom, dated April 6,1929, carton 6, Stephen H. Hart Library and Research Center, History Colorado Center.

235. Correspondence from 1933 to 1935, from Louise Hill to Mr. W.C. Shepherd (*Denver Post* manager and editor), carton 8, Stephen H. Hart Library and Research Center, History Colorado Center; correspondence from Louise Hill to Harry N. Rhoads (*Rocky Mountain News*), dated October 18, 1939, carton 8, Stephen H. Hart Library and Research Center, History Colorado Center.

236. Denver Public Library, "Polly Pry."

237. History Colorado Center, untitled newspaper article, undated, Louise Hill Scrapbook, carton 35, Stephen H. Hart Library and Research Center.

238. Ibid.

239. Ibid.

240. Bonniwell and Halaas, *History of the Denver Country Club*.

241. Ibid., 41.

242. History Colorado Center, "Society Dazzled by Tiara," "If You Just Must Be Good Take a Peep at These Suggestions" and "Crackers and Buttermilk Diet, Mrs. Hill Must Reduce Weight," undated, Louise Hill Scrapbook, carton 35, Stephen H. Hart Library and Research Center.

243. May, *Screening Out the Past*, 9.

244. History Colorado Center, "Society's Queen Owes Success to Human Qualities," undated, Louise Hill Scrapbook, carton 35, Stephen H. Hart Library and Research Center.

245. History Colorado Center, "The Box Occupants," undated, Louise Hill Scrapbook, carton 35, Stephen H. Hart Library and Research Center.
246. Homberger, *Mrs. Astor's New York*, 135.
247. Muccigrosso, "New York Has a Ball," 297–320; Beckert, *Monied Metropolis*, 1–2.
248. "Big Denver Society," *Rocky Mountain News*.
249. "Costumes for Arian Ball," *Denver Post*.
250. Melrose, "Mrs. Crawford Hill."
251. Marilyn Griggs Riley Papers, Louise Hill, manuscript. Box 2, FF32, Western History Genealogy Department, Denver Public Library.
252. Daugherty, "'Animal Dances.'"
253. Ibid.
254. Hill, "East vs. West," 44, 5.

Chapter 5

255. May, *Screening Out the Past*, 8
256. Ibid.
257. Ibid., 18
258. Ibid., 19
259. W. Rockwell, "Gentleman of Fortune," 17–18.
260. Ibid.
261. "Bulkeley Wells," *San Francisco Chronicle*.
262. Correspondence from Crawford Hill to Nathaniel Hill, dated March 21, 1919, Crawford Hill Collection, vol. 2, Western History Genealogy Department, Denver Public Library; correspondence from Crawford Hill to Nathaniel Hill, dated March 16, 1918, Crawford Hill Collection, vol. 2, Western History Genealogy Department, Denver Public Library.
263. Correspondence from Crawford Hill to Bulkeley Wells, dated November 23, 1920, Crawford Hill Collection, vol. 2, Western History Genealogy Department, Denver Public Library.
264. "Costumes for Arian Ball," *Denver Post*.
265. Riley, *High Altitude Attitudes*, 16.
266. Bancroft, interview.
267. Fetter, *Colorado's Legendary Lovers*, 103–6; correspondence between Crawford Hill, Nathaniel and Crawford Jr., Crawford Hill Collection, vol. 2, Western History Genealogy Department, Denver Public Library.

268. Correspondence from Nathaniel Hill to Louise Hill, dated April 25, 1912, carton 35, Stephen H. Hart Library and Research Center, History Colorado Center.

269. Correspondence from Nathaniel Hill to Louise Hill, dated March 17, 1912, carton 35, Stephen H. Hart Library and Research Center, History Colorado Center.

270. Correspondence from Nathaniel Hill to Louise Hill, dated Dec. 13, 1918, carton 35, Stephen H. Hart Library and Research Center, History Colorado Center.

271. Correspondence from Nathaniel Hill to Crawford Hill Jr., dated April 10, 1910, carton 35, Stephen H. Hart Library and Research Center, History Colorado Center.

272. Correspondence from Nathaniel Hill to Louise Hill, dated March 9, 1913, carton 35, Stephen H. Hart Library and Research Center, History Colorado Center.

273. W. Rockwell, "Gentleman of Fortune," 26.

274. Rockwell claims Crawford died of a stroke in his work "Gentleman of Fortune" (25). Griggs claims it was heart failure in *High Altitude Attitudes* (17).

275. "Bulkeley Wells," *Eagle Valley Enterprise*.

276. W. Rockwell, "Gentleman of Fortune," 27.

277. "Bulkeley Wells," *San Francisco Chronicle*.

278. Riley, *High Altitude Attitudes*, 17; Faulkner, *Ladies of the Brown*, part 2.

279. Monahan, "Bulkeley Wells."

Chapter 6

280. History Colorado Center, "The Hills Are to Bask in Royalty's Smile," undated, Louise Hill Scrapbook, carton 35, Stephen H. Hart Library and Research Center.

281. History Colorado Center, "Denver Society Woman to Enter Palace, Mrs. Crawford Hill Will Be 'Presented,'" undated, Louise Hill Scrapbook, carton 35, Stephen H. Hart Library and Research Center.

282. Ibid.

283. "Hill at British Court," *Denver Republican*.

284. Ibid.

285. History Colorado Center, "Denver Society Leader to Give Party March 13" and "Sacred Thirty-six of Denver Welcome Lord and Lady Decies,"

undated, Louise Hill Scrapbook, carton 35, Stephen H. Hart Library and Research Center.

286. *Rocky Mountain News*, October 3, 1911.

287. History Colorado Center, "Mrs. Hill Triumphs; Takes Lunch with Chinese Diplomat," undated, Louise Hill Scrapbook, carton 35, Stephen H. Hart Library and Research Center.

288. History Colorado Center, "Society Leader Meets Consul," undated, Louise Hill Scrapbook, carton 35, Stephen H. Hart Library and Research Center.

289. Correspondence from Elizabeth Gordon to Louise Hill, dated July 22, 1909, Stephen H. Hart Library and Research Center, History Colorado Center.

290. Correspondence from Crawford Hill to George W. Gano Esquire, dated September 19, 1919, no. 435, Crawford Hill Collection, vol. 2, Western History Genealogy Department, Denver Public Library.

291. Ibid.

292. The incident at the country club took place on August 9, and by August 18, Louise was in Memphis, Tennessee, as letter no. 423 in the Crawford Hill collection, vol. 2 is a letter from Crawford to her in Memphis.

293. Denver Country Club, articles of incorporation, bylaws, rules, officers, and members of the Denver Country Club, dated 1926, 52

294. Ibid., 54.

295. Bancroft, interview.

296. Bonniwell and Halaas, *History of the Denver Country Club*, 59.

297. Ibid.

298. "Hill Helped Crystallize," *Denver Post*.

Chapter 7

299. "Society as an Art," *Denver Post*,

300. "Hill Helped Crystallize," *Denver Post*.

301. History Colorado Center, untitled newspaper article, undated, Louise Hill Scrapbook, carton 35, Stephen H. Hart Library and Research Center.

302. Western History Genealogy Department, agreement of sale for 969 Sherman Street, March 28, 1947, Jack Weil Collection, Box 1, Denver Public Library.

303. Melrose, "Auctioneer's Hammer."

304. Ibid.

305. Correspondence from Louise Hill to Mary Robinson, dated September 20, 1938, Louise Hill Collection, box 10, FF367, Stephen H. Hart Library and Research Center, History Colorado Center.

306. Correspondence from Louise Hill to Nathaniel and Crawford Hill, dated August 28, 1940, Louise Hill Collection, box 10, FF367, Stephen H. Hart Library and Research Center, History Colorado Center.

307. Correspondence from Louise Hill to Nathaniel and Crawford Hill, dated August 23, 1940, Louise Hill Collection, box 10, FF367, Stephen H. Hart Library and Research Center, History Colorado Center.

308. Denver Public Library, Last will and testament of Louise Sneed Hill. Jack Weil Collection, box 1, Western History Genealogy Department.

309. Findagrave, Berkeley Memorial Cemetery in Middletown, Rhode Island, www.findagrave.com.

310. Kreck, *Rich People*, 169.

311. History Colorado Center, untitled newspaper article, undated, Louise Hill Scrapbook, carton 35, Stephen H. Hart Library and Research Center.

312. Melrose, "Auctioneer's Hammer."

313. Marranzino, "Rich Memories"; *Historic Denver News*, "Leader of the 'Sacred 36.'"

314. "Society as an Art," *Denver Post*.

315. "Hill—Arbiter," *Denver Post*.

316. Morris, "Society Defended by Mrs. Hill," 5.

317. History Colorado Center, "Mrs. Crawford Hill, Sculptor," undated, Louise Hill Scrapbook, carton 35, Stephen H. Hart Library and Research Center.

318. Allard, "Mrs. Crawford Hill."

319. Marranzino, "Rich Memories."

320. "Hill Fined as Smuggler," *Sun*.

321. "Veteran Member," *Denver Post*; "Plays Nurse," *Denver Post*; "Arrives with Son," *Denver Post*; Price, interview.

322. "Longest Parade," *Rocky Mountain News*; "Thomas Denounced," *Denver Post*.

323. "Denver Society Women," *Denver Post*.

324. Morris, "Society Defended by Mrs. Hill," 5.

325. Price, interview.

326. Marranzino, "Rich Memories."

BIBLIOGRAPHY

Untitled newspaper articles from the Louise Sneed Hill collection scrapbook, carton 35, *History Colorado Center.*

Titled newspaper articles from the Louise Sneed Hill collection scrapbook, carton 35, *History Colorado Center.*
- "The Box Occupants"
- "Crackers and Buttermilk Diet, Mrs. Hill Must Reduce Weight"
- "Denver's Most Exclusive Set Ruled by One"
- "Denver Society Leader to Give Party March 13"
- "Denver Society Woman to Enter Palace, Mrs. Crawford Hill Will Be 'Presented'"
- "The Hills Are to Bask in Royalty's Smile"
- "Hill-Sneed Wedding"
- "If You Just Must Be Good Take a Peep at These Suggestions"
- "Mrs. Crawford Hill, Sculptor."
- "Mrs. Hill Triumphs; Takes Lunch with Chinese Diplomat"
- "Sacred Thirty-Six of Denver Welcome Lord and Lady Decies"
- "Society Dazzled by Tiara"
- "Society Forecasts"
- "Society Leader Meets Consul"
- "Society's Queen Owes Success to Human Qualities"
- "Who Are the Mighty Ninety?"

Abbot, Carl, Stephen J. Leonard and Thomas J. Noel. *Colorado: A History of the Centennial State*. Boulder: University Press of Colorado, 2013.

Alexander, Brian. "The Rich Are Different—and Not in a Good Way, Studies Suggest." Aired by NBC News on August 10, 2011.

Allard, Leola. "Mrs. Crawford Hill." Louise Hill scrapbook, undated, Carton 35, Stephen H. Hart Library and Research Center, History Colorado Center.

Allen, Robert C. *Horrible Prettiness: Burlesque and American Culture*. Chapel Hill: University of North Carolina Press, 1991.

Ancestry. "Marriage bond, Louisa Bethel and William Morgan Sneed, dated June 28, 1842." North Carolina Marriage Records, 1741–2011. www.ancestry.com.

———. "Marriages of Granville County, North Carolina, 1753–1868." www.ancestry.com.

———. "Rhode Island, Marriage Index, 1851–1920." www.search.ancestry.com.

Andrews, Thomas G. *Killing for Coal: America's Deadliest Labor War*. Cambridge, MA: Harvard University Press, 2008.

Anonymous. "Crawford Hill." In *Men and Women of Colorado Past and Present in One Volume*. Denver, CO: Pioneer Publishing CO, 1944.

———. "St. Mary's School." *Churchman* 94 (September 29, 1906): 459.

Appleton, J.H. "Hon. Nathaniel P. Hill '56." *Brown Alumni Monthly*, 1900.

Aspen Daily Times. "Crawford Hill Married." January 16, 1895.

Ayers, Edward L. *The Promise of the New South: Life After Reconstruction*. New York: Oxford University Press, 2007.

Bakken, Gordon Morris, and Brenda Farrington. *Encyclopedia of Women in the American West*. Thousand Oaks, CA: Sage Publications, 2003.

Bancroft, Caroline. Interview by Sandra Dallas Atchison and James H. Davis, July 22, 1971. Two cassettes, Caroline Bancroft Collection, Series 4 Audio-Visual, AVBox 1, Western History Genealogy Department, Denver Public Library.

Beaton, Gail M. *Colorado Women: A History*. Boulder: University of Colorado Press, 2012.

Beckert, Sven. *Monied Metropolis*. Cambridge: Cambridge University Press, 2001.

Bethell, Mary Jeffreys. "July 27th Sunday" in "Diary January 1st—December 1865" in *Documenting the American South*. Chapel Hill: Southern Historical Collection at the University of North Carolina, Chapel Hill.

Bibby, Emily Katherine. "Making the American Aristocracy: Women, Cultural Capital, and High Society in New York City, 1870–1900." Master's thesis, Virginia Polytechnic Institute and State University, 2009.

Biographical Directory of the United States Congress. "Hill, Nathaniel Peter." www.bioguide.congress.gov.

Blumin, Stuart M. *The Emergence of the Middle Class: Social Experience in the American City, 1760–1900.* New York: Cambridge University Press, 1989.

Bond, Beverly G., and Janann Sherman. *Memphis: In Black and White.* Charleston, SC: Arcadia Publishing, 2003.

Bonniwell, Chuck, and David Fridtjof Halaas. *The History of the Denver Country Club, 1887–2006.* Sarasota, FL: Oceanview Books, 2006.

Breger, Carpel L. "Two Replies to Mr. Eilers," *Financial World* 35, no.1 (January 3, 1921): 553.

Bushman, Richard. *The Refinement of Class in America: Persons, Houses, Cities.* New York: Vintage Books, 1992.

Cashman, Sean Dennis. *America in the Gilded Age.* 3rd ed. New York: New York University Press, 1993.

City of Denver Building Permit No. 1070, dated August 15, 1902.

City of Denver Building Permit No. 1071, dated September 5, 1901.

Correspondence from A. Piatt Andrews to Louise Hill, dated March 4, 1918. Louise Hill scrapbook, carton 35, Stephen H. Hart Library and Research Center, History Colorado Center.

Correspondence from Crawford Hill to Bulkeley Wells, dated November 23, 1920. Crawford Hill Collection, vol. 2, Western History Genealogy Department, Denver Public Library.

Correspondence from Crawford Hill to George W. Gano Esquire, dated September 19, 1919. No. 435, Crawford Hill Collection, vol. 2, Western History Genealogy Department, Denver Public Library.

Correspondence from Crawford Hill to James A. Rose, Esq., dated March 27, 1900. Crawford Hill Collection, vol. 1, Western History Genealogy Department, Denver Public Library.

Correspondence from Crawford Hill to Louise Hill, dated August 18, 1919. No. 423, Crawford Hill Collection, vol. 2, Western History Genealogy Department, Denver Public Library.

Correspondence from Crawford Hill to Nathaniel Hill, dated March 16, 1918. Crawford Hill Collection, vol. 2, Western History Genealogy Department, Denver Public Library.

Correspondence from Crawford Hill to Nathaniel Hill, dated March 21, 1919. Crawford Hill Collection, vol. 2, Western History Genealogy Department, Denver Public Library.

Correspondence from Elizabeth Gordon to Louise Hill, dated July 22, 1909. Stephen H. Hart Library and Research Center, History Colorado Center.

Correspondence from Louise Hill to Mary Robinson, dated September 20, 1938. Louise Hill Collection, box 10, FF367, Stephen H. Hart Library and Research Center, History Colorado Center.

Correspondence from Louise Hill to Miss Helen Eastom, dated April 6,1929. Carton 6, Stephen H. Hart Library and Research Center, History Colorado Center.

Correspondence from Louise Hill to Mr. Harry N. Rhoads (*Rocky Mountain News*), dated October 18, 1939. Carton 8, Stephen H. Hart Library and Research Center, History Colorado Center.

Correspondence from Louise Hill to Mrs. H.H. Tammen, dated March 4, 1927. Carton 11, Stephen H. Hart Library and Research Center, History Colorado Center.

Correspondence from Louise Hill to Mr. W.C. Shepherd (*Denver Post* manager and editor), dated July 15, 1933. Carton 8, Stephen H. Hart Library and Research Center, History Colorado Center.

Correspondence from Louise Hill to Mr. W.C. Shepherd (*Denver Post* manager and editor), dated May 5, 1934. Carton 8, Stephen H. Hart Library and Research Center, History Colorado Center.

Correspondence from Louise Hill to Mr. W.C. Shepherd (*Denver Post* manager and editor), dated August 1, 1935. Carton 8, Stephen H. Hart Library and Research Center, History Colorado Center.

Correspondence from Louise Hill to Nathaniel and Crawford Hill, dated August 23, 1940. Louise Hill Collection, box 10, FF367, Stephen H. Hart Library and Research Center, History Colorado Center.

Correspondence from Louise Hill to Nathaniel and Crawford Hill, dated August 28, 1940. Louise Hill Collection, box 10, FF367, Stephen H. Hart Library and Research Center, History Colorado Center.

Correspondence from Nathaniel Hill to Crawford Hill Jr., dated April 10, 1910. Carton 35, Stephen H. Hart Library and Research Center, History Colorado Center.

Correspondence from Nathaniel Hill to Louise Hill, dated March 17, 1912. Carton 35, Stephen H. Hart Library and Research Center, History Colorado Center.

Correspondence from Nathaniel Hill to Louise Hill, dated April 25, 1912. Carton 35, Stephen H. Hart Library and Research Center, History Colorado Center.

Correspondence from Nathaniel Hill to Louise Hill, dated March 9, 1913. Carton 35, Stephen H. Hart Library and Research Center, History Colorado Center.

Correspondence from Nathaniel Hill to Louise Hill, dated December 13, 1918. Carton 35, Stephen H. Hart Library and Research Center, History Colorado Center.

Daugherty, Greg. "The 'Animal Dances' So Wild They Were Banned from the White House." History Stories. www.history.com.

Denver Country Club. Articles of incorporation, bylaws, rules, officers, and members of the Denver Country Club, dated 1926.

Denver Post. "Announcement: The Foo-Wing Herb Co. Comes to Denver: The Greatest Combination of Oriental Physicians in the World. Some Statement of What It Is and What It Does." July 23, 1911.

———. "Arrival of Mr. and Mrs. Hill." February 1, 1895.

———. "Colorado Patriots Open Purses to Swell Soldier's Family Fund: Mr. and Mrs. Crawford Hill Treble Contribution for Aid of Those Dependent on Men Who Must Fight for Nation." April 10, 1917.

———. "Coming Events." August 25, 1906.

———. "Costumes for Arian Ball Surpass All Imagination." April 11, 1912.

———. "Denver Society Women May Go as Delegates to Big Convention." February 3,1916.

———. "Europe Has Fewer Snobs Than America." 1926.

———. "Mrs. Brown Climbs into '36' Crowd; Guest at Luncheon." May 2, 1912.

———. "Mrs. Crawford Hill—Arbiter of the 'Sacred 36.'" Part of Fairmount Cemetery's collection on Pioneer Coloradans.

———. "Mrs. Crawford Hill Arrives with Son." April 30, 1930.

———. "Mrs. Crawford Hill Fractures Her Wrist," January 19, 1908.

———. "Mrs. Hill Helped Crystallize Denver Society in Early '90s." May 30, 1955.

———. "Mrs. Hill Plays Nurse for Old-Time Servant at Ordeal in Hospital." December 20, 1916.

———. "Society as an Art: The Portrait of a Lady." Febuary 21, 1930.

———. "Society Page." May 2, 1912.

———. "Thomas Denounced in Scathing Tone by Woman Envoy." October 25, 1914.

———. "Veteran Member of Crawford Hill Household Dies." April 28, 1930.

———. "Weds a Southern Belle." September 1, 1895.

———. "Who's Who Social Arc and Tallow Dips Are All Listed in the Red Book of Denver's Society." June 10, 1908.

Denver Public Library. Last will and testament of Louise Sneed Hill. Jack Weil Collection, box 1, Western History Genealogy Department.

Denver Public Library. "Polly Pry." Genealogy, African American and Western History Resources. www.history.denverlibrary.org.

Denver Republican. "Mrs. Crawford Hill at British Court." July 6, 1907.

DuBois, W.E.B. *Black Reconstruction in America, 1860–1880.* New York: Free Press, 1998.

Eagle Valley Enterprise. "Bulkeley Wells, Suicide, Once Colorful Figure in Colorado." June 5, 1931.

Eastom, Helen. "Hospitality of Mrs. Hill World Famed." *Denver Post,* September 12, 1926.

Faulkner, Debra B. *Ladies of the Brown: A Women's History of Denver's Most Elegant Hotel.* Charleston, SC: The History Press, 2010.

Fell, James E. "Nathaniel P. Hill: A Scientist-Entrepreneur in Colorado." *Arizona and the West* 15, no. 4 (1973): 315–32. www.jstor.org.

———. *Ores to Metals: The Rocky Mountain Smelting Industry.* Lincoln: University of Nebraska Press, 1979.

Ferril, Thomas Hornsby. Interviewed by Marilyn Griggs Riley, June 21, 1983.

Ferril, William Columbus. "Crawford Hill." In *Sketches of Colorado: Being an Analytical Summary and Biographical History of the State of Colorado as Portrayed in the Lives of the Pioneers, the Founders, the Builders, the Statesmen, and the Prominent and Progressive Citizens who Helped in the Development and History Making of Colorado.* Vol. 1. Denver, CO: Western Press Bureau Co., 1911.

Fetter, Rosemary. *Colorado's Legendary Lovers: Historical Heartthrobs and Haunting Romances.* Golden, CO: Fulcrum Publishing, 2004.

Fink, Leon. *The Long Gilded Age: American Capitalism and the Lessons of a New World Order.* Philadelphia: University of Pennsylvania Press, 2015.

Fisher, Ellen. Alice Hale Hill Collection Forward. Collection 308, Stephen H. Hart Library and Research Center, History Colorado Center.

Foner, Eric. *A Short History of Reconstruction, 1863–1877.* New York: HarperCollins, 1990.

Fourth Estate. "Former Prominent Denver Publisher Is Dead." December 30, 1922.

Fowles, Susan S., and Susan S. Toules. "Col. Richard Henderson of the Famous Transylvania Company." *Register of Kentucky State Historical Society* 7, no. 20 (1909): 37–45. www.jstor.org.

Gibson, Scott M. *A.J. Gordon: American Premillennialist.* Lanham, MD: University Press of America, 2001.

Gordon, Linda. *The Great Arizona Orphan Abduction.* Cambridge, MA: Harvard University Press, 1999.

Gresham, John M. *Biographical Cyclopedia of the Commonwealth of Kentucky: Embracing Biographies of Many of the Prominent Men and Families of the State.* Chicago, IL: J. M. Gresham Company, 1896.

Griggs, Marilyn. "Louise Sneed Hill: She Scandalized Denver's Old Guard," *Colorado Homes & Lifestyles* 6 (1986).

Halttunen, Karen. *Confidence Men and Painted Women: A Study of Middle-Class Culture in America, 1830–1870.* New Haven, CT: Yale University Press, 1982.

Harper, Ida Husted, and Susan B. Anthony, ed. *History of Woman Suffrage.* Vol. 4. Rochester, NY: Self-published, 1902.

Haywood, William D. *Big Bill Haywood: The Autobiography of William D. Haywood.* New York: International Publishers Co., 1929.

Headley, Russel. *The History of Orange County, New York.* Middletown, NY: Van Duesen and Elms, 1908.

Henderson Gold Leaf. "Social and Personal." December 10, 1891.

Herald Democrat. "Without Any Display: Funeral of Ex-Senator Hill Was Private According to His Desire." May 25, 1900.

Hill-Hold and Brick House Museums. "Museum History." www.hillholdandbrickhouse.org.

Hill, Mrs. Crawford. "East vs. West." *Harper's Bazaar*, May 1910.

Hill, Nathaniel P. "Nathaniel P. Hill Inspects Colorado: Letters Written in 1864." *Colorado Magazine* 33, no. 4 (October 1956).

Historic Denver News. "As the Leader of the 'Sacred 36,' She Could Make or Break Someone." May 1977.

Historic Memphis. "The Mayors of Memphis from 1827 to Present." www.historic-memphis.com.

Homberger, Eric. *Mrs. Astor's New York: Money and Social Power in a Gilded Age.* New Haven, CT: Yale University Press, 2002.

Hull, William T. "Hill, Nathaniel Peter." In *American National Biography*. New York: Oxford University Press, 2000.

Inter Ocean. "At the Altar." October 28, 1888.

Iversen, Kristen. *Molly Brown: Unraveling the Myth.* Boulder, CO: Big Earth Publishing, 1999.

Kania, Alan J. *The Denver Press Club: 150 Years of Printer's Devils, Bohemians, and Ghosts.* Bloomington, IN: Xlibris Corporation, 2018.

King, Greg. *A Season of Splendor: The Court of Mrs. Astor in Gilded Age New York.* Hoboken, NJ: John Wiley & Sons, 2009.

Kreck, Dick. *Rich People Behaving Badly.* Golden, CO: Fulcrum Publishing, 2016.

Lee, Heath Hardage. *Winnie Davis: Daughter of the Lost Cause.* Lincoln, NE: Potomac Books, 2014.

Leonard, John W. *Woman's Who's Who of America: A Biographical Dictionary of Contemporary Women of the United States and Canada.* New York: American Commonwealth Company, 1915.

Limerick, Patricia Nelson. *A Ditch in Time: The City, the West, and Water.* Golden, CO: Fulcrum Publishing, 2012.

MacColl, Gail, and Carol McD. Wallace. *To Marry and English Lord.* New York: Workman Publishing, 1989.

Marilyn Griggs Riley Papers. Alice Hale Hill, manuscript. Box 2, FF32, Western History Genealogy Department, Denver Public Library.

———. Louise Hill, manuscript. Box 2, FF32, Western History Genealogy Department, Denver Public Library.

———. WH2101. Box 2, FF30-32. Denver Public Library.

Marranzino, Pasquale. "Mrs. Hill Leaves Rich Memories." *Rocky Mountain News,* June 1, 1955.

Matthiessen, F.O. *American Renaissance: Art and Expression in the Age of Emerson and Whitman.* New York: Oxford University Press, 1941.

May, Larry. *Screening Out the Past: The Birth of Mass Culture and the Motion Picture Industry.* New York: Oxford University Press, 1983.

McPherson, James M. *Battle Cry of Freedom: The Civil War Era.* New York: Oxford University Press, 1988.

Melrose, Frances. "The Auctioneer's Hammer Falls on the Past: Fine Old Furnishings of the Crawford Hill Mansion Bring Eager Bids." *Rocky Mountain News,* May 20, 1947.

———. "Mrs. Crawford Hill: Dowager Queen of Denver Society." *Rocky Mountain News,* May 4, 1947.

Memphis Daily Appeal. "Law Firm." June 13, 1873.

———. "Mont Eagle Springs: A Delightful Resort, Where All Take the Appeal—The Ball of the Season." August 16, 1881.

Military History Online. "William Morgan Sneed." www.militaryhistoryonline. com.

Mitchell, Martha. "Nathaniel P. Hill." In *Encyclopedia Brunoniana.* Providence, RI: Brown University, 1993.

Monahan, Kaspar. "Bulkeley Wells Spent and Lost Huge Fortunes, Gambled $15,000,000 for Harry Payne Whitney and Failed." *Rocky Mountain News,* May 27, 1931.

Morris, Mildred. "Society Defended by Mrs. Hill: Not Immoral, Leader Declares." *Rocky Mountain News,* April 15, 1914.

Muccigrosso, Robert. "New York Has a Ball: The Bradley Martin Extravaganza." *New York History* 75, no. 3 (1994): 297–320. www.jstor.org.

National Archives. Records of the commissary general of prisoners, record group 249. Selected records of the War Department relating to Confederate prisoners of war, 1861–65 (National Archives microfilm publication M598, 145 rolls). Washington, D.C.

National Archives and Records Administration. Consolidated lists of Civil War draft registration records (Provost Marshal General's Bureau, consolidated enrollment lists, 1863–65). Record group: 110, collection name: consolidated enrollment lists, 1863–65 (Civil War Union Draft Records), NAI: 4213514, archive volume number: 1 of 3. Washington, D.C.

NCGenweb Project and North Carolina. "Sneed Plantation." www.ncgenweb.us.

New York Times. "A Memphis Lawyer Insane." October 22, 1892.

———. "Mrs. Astor's Annual Ball: About Three Hundred Guests Attended the Beautiful Function." January 30, 1900.

———. "Mrs. Astor's Final Dinner: A Farewell Entertainment Preparatory to Her Trip to Europe at Her Fifth Avenue Home." January 28, 1898.

———. "Mrs. William Astor's Ball: Society People Attend in Throngs After Listening to Grand Opera." January 18, 1898.

Noel, Thomas J. *The City and the Saloon: Denver, 1858–1916.* Lincoln: University of Nebraska Press, 1982.

Omaha Bee. "Telegraphic Briefs." January 18, 1895.

Oxford Dictionary, s.v. "nouveau riche." www.lexico.com.

Oxford Public Ledger. "Traveling Around: Paragraphic Mention of People Who Are Coming and Going." December 25, 1891.

Pace, Mark. Interviewed by Shelby Carr. September 6, 2019.

Papers of Pickney C. and William D. Bethell, 1848–1901. "Biography of William D. Bethell, 1840–1906." Library of the State Historical Society of Colorado.

Peace, Samuel Thomas. *"Zeb's Black Baby," Vance County, North Carolina: A Short History.* Vance County, NC: Seeman Printery, 1956.

Price, Nina. Interviewed by Marilyn Griggs Riley, June 10, 1984.

Pueblo Chieftain. "Captain Bethel Dies in Denver." August 20, 1906.

Pulkrabek, Payton, "The New Middle Class in the Gilded Age (2016)." Curriculum Unit on the Gilded Age in the United States. www.repository.stcloudstate.edu.

Raleigh North Carolina Semi-Weekly News. "Latest News—The Situation." September 30, 1864.

———. October 9, 1864.

Raleigh Register. "Deaths." July 23, 1862.

Register of Deaths in the City of Memphis, Tennessee. File no. 49560, 71.

Richardson, Heather Cox. *West from Appomattox: The Reconstruction of America after the Civil War*. New Haven, CT: Yale University Press, 2007.

Richmond Dispatch. "Personal Points." June 6, 1886.

Riley, Marilyn Griggs. *High Altitude Attitudes: Six Savvy Colorado Women*. Boulder, CO: Big Earth Publishing, 2006.

Rockman, Seth. *Scraping By: Wage Labor, Slavery, and Survival in Early Baltimore*. Baltimore: Johns Hopkins University Press, 2009.

Rockwell, Mary Rech. "Gender Transformations: The Gilded Age and the Roaring Twenties." *OAH Magazine of History* 19, no. 2 (2005).

Rockwell, Wilson. "Gentleman of Fortune." In *The 1966 Brand Book*. edited by William D. Powell, vol. 22. Denver: Denver Westerners Inc., 1967.

Rocky Mountain News. "Afternoon Tea." August 23, 1891.

———. "Around the Tea Table." July 2, 1893

———. "Babies' Summer Hospital." May 11, 1897.

———. "Big Denver Society Ball Is Scheduled for Spring." January 14, 1912.

———. "Club to Greet Marshall." October 30, 1917.

———. "Denver Motor Club Gets New Quarters." December 23, 1908.

———. "Denver's Longest Parade." November 16, 1915.

———. "Mrs. Davis Relative Mrs. Crawford Hill." October 17, 1906

———. October 3, 1911.

———. "Our Central Gold Region—The Pike's Peak Mining District." September 7, 1860.

———. "Sacred Thirty-Six." April 22, 1934.

Rohe, Alice. "Society as a Fine Art." *Rocky Mountain News*, February 2, 1913.

Rosner, David. "Portrait of an Unhealthy City: New York in the 1800s." Living City/NYC. www.banhdc.org.

San Francisco Chronicle. "Bulkeley Wells, Noted Mining Engineer, Commits Suicide in S.F. Office." May 27, 1931.

Scobey, David. "Anatomy of the Promenade: The Politics of Bourgeois Sociability in Nineteenth-Century New York." *Social History* 17, no. 2 (1992): 203–27.

Semple, James Alexander. "Mrs. N.P. Hill." In *Representative Women of Colorado*, 2nd ed. Denver: Williamson-Haffner Company, 1914.

Stansell, Christine. *City of Women: Sex and Class in New York, 1789–1860*. New York: Alfred A. Knopf Inc., 1982.

Steele, B.W. "Honorable Nathaniel Peter Hill: Ex-United States Senator of Colorado." In *National Magazine: A Journal Devoted to American History*. Vol. 15. New York: National History Company, 1891.

St. John's Episcopal Church. "St. John's Episcopal Church pamphlet, Williamsboro, NC." www.archive.org.

Stone, Wilbur Fiske. "Nathaniel Peter Hill." In *History of Colorado*, vol. 4. Chicago: S.J. Clarke Publishing Company, 1919.

Sun (New York). "Mrs. Hill Fined as Smuggler: Wife of Denver Capitalist Pleads Guilty and Pays $300." June 24, 1913.

Tarborough Southerner. "A Daughter of Jeff Davis in the State." September 10, 1875.

Thayer, William Makepeace. "Thomas H. Lawrence." In *Marvels of the New West: A Vivid Portrayal of the Stupendous Marvels in the Vast Wonderland West of the Missouri River.* Norwich, CT: Henry Bill Publishing Company, 1887.

Times Picayune (New Orleans, LA). "Sneed-Hill." January 16, 1895.

Torchlight. "Death of Mrs. S.A. Sneed." January 22, 1878.

Trachtenberg, Alan. *The Incorporation of America: Culture and Society in the Gilded Age.* New York: Hill and Wang, 1982.

Tribune. "Letter to the Editor." September 11, 1875.

United States Census Bureau. "Why can't I find 1890 census records?" www.census.gov.

University of North Carolina at Chapel Hill. Subseries 6.1. parochial visits, 1870–99, in the Pettigrew family papers no. 592. Southern Historical Collection, Wilson Library.

University of North Carolina at Chapel Hill. Volume 2: Diary, 1890–93, in the Goodrich Wilson Marrow papers, no. 1723. Southern Historical Collection, Wilson Library.

University of North Florida. "Brochure: Hotel St. Elmo, Green Cove Springs, Florida." Tourism. www.digitalcommons.unf.edu.

Van Rensselaer, May King and Frederic Van De Water. *The Social Ladder.* New York: Henry Holt and Company, 1924.

Wecter, Dixon. *The Saga of American Society a Record of Social Aspiration 1607–1937.* New York: Charles Scribner's Sons, 1937.

West, Elliot. *The Contested Plains: Indians, Goldseekers and the Rush to Colorado.* Topeka: University Press of Kansas, 1998.

Western History Genealogy Department. Agreement of sale for 969 Sherman Street, March 28, 1947. Jack Weil Collection, Box 1, Denver Public Library.

White, B.S. "Lucius M. Cuthbert." *Representative Men of the West in Caricature* 1, no. 1 (1904).

White, Richard. *It's Your Misfortune and None of My Own: A New History of the American West*. Norman: University of Oklahoma Press, 1991.

———. *The Republic for Which It Stands: The United States During Reconstruction and the Gilded Age, 1865–1896*. New York: Oxford University Press, 2017.

Who's Who in Denver Society, 1908. Denver: W.H. Kistler Stationary Co., 1908.

Wilentz, Sean. *Chants Democratic: New York City and the Rise of the American Working Class, 1788–1850*. New York: Oxford University Press, 1984; repr. 2004.

Williams, Wiley J. "Transylvania Company." Encyclopedia of North Carolina. www.ncpedia.org.

Yuma Pioneer. "Death of Senator Hill." May 25, 1900.

INDEX

ABOUT THE AUTHOR

Shelby Carr graduated from the University of Colorado with a master's degree in American history with a minor in public history and a certificate in historic preservation. She also has a genealogical research certificate from Boston University and a certificate in antiques, collectibles and appraising from Asheford Institute of Antiques. Shelby specializes in Gilded Age women's history and has had four articles published that pertain to the subject of her master's thesis and, now, full-length work, Louise Sneed Hill.

Visit us at
www.historypress.com